THE NATIONAL TRUST BOOK OF
The Farm

THE NATIONAL TRUST BOOK OF
The Farm

Gillian Darley

with photographs by
Pamla Toler

The National Trust
Weidenfeld & Nicolson

Contents

Text © Gillian Darley 1981
Photographs © Pamla Toler 1981

The National Trust Book of The Farm
was conceived, edited and designed
by Frances Lincoln Limited for:

The National Trust
42 Queen Anne's Gate, London SW1
and
George Weidenfeld and Nicolson Limited
91 Clapham High Street, London SW4

ISBN 0 297 78006 9

Printed in Great Britain by Jolly & Barber Limited, Rugby

Half title page: Trentishoe, North Devon. *Title page*: Farm near Chipping
Norton, on the Oxfordshire and Warwickshire borders. *This page*: Tithe barn,
Lenham, Kent.

Author's Acknowledgments

I owe very many thanks to a considerable number of people. I hope all those whom I have troubled for information over the last months, and who gave me help and encouragement, will include themselves in this general vote of thanks. However, I would like to single out a few people for their extra help: Eileen Harris and John Popham for handing over their theses and trusting me with them for months on end; John and Jane Penoyre and Michael Barker for help in finding specific locations; David Pearce, Secretary of the Society for the Protection of Ancient Buildings, for allowing me to pursue the subject of farm buildings on the Barns Working Party of the SPAB; Bill Drummond of the Covent Garden Gallery for bringing to my attention a stream of wonderful images of farm buildings in pencil, watercolour and oil; Nigel Harvey, for reading and making infinitely valuable comments on the manuscript; and Susan Berry, my editor, for calm and good sense in my moments of panic.

Finally, I would like to offer particular thanks to Pamla Toler for the photographs of the buildings themselves, making this book of the present and not of the misty, distant past. We have both, on our respective travels, met and talked to innumerable farmers, landowners, architects, planners, chartered surveyors, and land agents, as well as many people who live amidst farmland and farm buildings. Many of them value the farm buildings that make such a fine contribution to the landscape of England and Wales. This book, however, is dedicated to those who remain unconverted, that they may look once again at their surroundings and temper their expedient view of the present with a proper respect for the past.

February 1981.

Picture Acknowledgments

All the contemporary photographs, taken during the last two years, are the work of Pamla Toler with the exception of those appearing on the following pages: p. 42 bottom, p. 44, p. 46, p. 62, p. 86, pp. 90–1, p. 93, p. 105 bottom right, p. 109, p. 112 top, p. 123 top, pp. 138–9, p. 143 bottom, p. 205 © Gillian Darley; p. 81, pp. 134–5, pp. 152–3, p. 196, p. 199, p. 200, p. 228 © Edward Piper; and p. 201 © Roger Hillier.

The Publishers would also like to thank the following for permission to reproduce photographs from their collections:

The Architectural Review (Eric de Maré) p. 96; Cheltenham Art Gallery & Museum Service p. 16 top; Country Life p. 29; A. F. Kersting p. 51 top; National Monuments Record p. 30 top, p. 38, p. 51 bottom, p. 57, p. 58, p. 156, p. 172–3, p. 188; Science Museum, London p. 16 bottom, p. 82 top; and The Trustees of Sir John Soane's Museum p. 37.

The Library of the Royal Agricultural Society of England kindly loaned copies of *The Farmer's Guide* by Arthur Young and *Farm Homesteads of England* by J. Bailey Denton for photography, and William Drummond, Covent Garden Gallery Ltd, provided the photograph of a painting by Robert Hills of a Kent farmyard (p. 82 bottom).

Introduction

The evolution of the farm is, to a large extent, the mirror of the economic and social history of this country. It deals with changes in land ownership, the shift from self-sufficiency to a centralized economy and transformations wrought by industrialization and standardization. In purely architectural terms, it covers the move away from local skills and traditions in building towards professional expertise, and the pursuit of fashion or, at least, the established norm in design.

It is hard to disassociate the farm from rural nostalgia, an exclusively urban product. Yet even the most picturesque, Beatrix Potter-like farm was designed for smooth functioning rather than aesthetic appeal. The whole farmstead was, essentially, a carefully balanced economic unit, with both animals and crops contributing to a measured cycle. Only recently has the perpetuity of that cycle been broken. High land values and heavy capital costs require good returns in the shape of high yields obtained by intensive methods (now based on quotas reflecting the dictates of the agricultural policy of the Common Market). All this has led to a form of agriculture in which specialization tends to make each process increasingly isolated from the next. The new buildings reflect that fact.

Yet it was the traditional cycle, as well as the interconnecting threads between geology, landscape, site, materials and the built farmstead, that gave the older buildings their intriguing logic. As methods of farming changed, the connections shifted and the buildings changed accordingly.

As we notice the pinpricks of the bright white farmsteads on the green hillsides of the Lake District or the stark black weather-boarding of an Essex barn set against the changing brown, green or gold of its surroundings, the connection between buildings and the setting is entirely harmonious and logical – if we follow it through. For farm buildings and the farmhouse itself are functional structures and their beauty arises from the natural wisdom that governed their construction, adaptation and, even, reconstruction.

Farm buildings are the *leitmotif* of the countryside. It seems appropriate to describe them with a musical term for they are thematic, and the resonance of their forms, colours and textures within the scenery is that of sound, overall and orchestrated. Here and there is the solo instrument, spectacular in its own right, but much more important is the orchestral effect.

Dependent on the land for their function as well as for their materials, farm buildings have, over the centuries, been integral to their particular setting; indeed it is impossible to envisage many stretches of landscape without their accompanying ranges of buildings. We expect them to be there as we expect the rising outline of the church spire, the knolls of beeches on the Downs or the horizon as we approach the sea. So, too, perhaps without thinking much about it, we expect the countryside to tell us about itself through its farm buildings; their shape and site have a tale to tell, as do their timber, stone and brick. Owing to the many changes that have occurred in the development of agriculture, and consequently in the buildings, from the late medieval period onwards, the tale is a complex one. To appreciate the existence of the traditional farm buildings in the landscape is one thing, to understand how they developed is quite another.

Because this is a book about existing farm buildings, both those in the vernacular tradition, using the materials of the locality, and the architect- and engineer-designed farmsteads of the last 200 years, it begins, properly speaking, during the Tudor period. From the late sixteenth century onwards, we can begin to build up a picture of the buildings of the farm, that is to say, the farmhouse and the related farm buildings. Anything that has survived from an earlier period is atypical, the product of extravagant wealth or exceptional skills. Medieval tithe barns are still standing because of their architectural excellence and because of their scale – which has had such an impact on the landscape. Nothing of such dimensions had been built in the countryside before – little, until recent years, since.

The history of farm buildings is the history of change. It is thought that some Cornish farms, for example, stand on the sites of Iron Age farmsteads – yet the evidence exists only in the site, and perhaps in a boulder or two taken into a wall some centuries after Domesday. However, even the most stream-lined of farming ventures usually operates in and around a fair number of older buildings, perhaps converted, perhaps somewhat underused. Certain of these are standing because their design and materials embody basic truths about the way in which buildings work; too many of the modern substitutes have failed to live up to their promise. Others still stand because they are of exceptional architectural or historical worth, while others remain because they are of sufficient beauty, either individually or in their setting, to persuade their owners to preserve them – even at the cost of some efficiency.

The number of farms is falling (by 4 per cent between 1975 and 1979); the number of people engaged in farming has dropped by over 18 per cent in the last ten years. These figures hide hard facts: deserted farm buildings (resulting from amalgamation), farmhouses no longer owned by farmers, and empty farm cottages. Many of these buildings, whether still attached to working farms or obsolete in their entirety, represent a massive waste of resources, in terms of building materials and of potentially useful space. Nobody should attempt to underestimate the difficulties, nor the scale of the problem, but certainly they cannot be ignored.

Until very recent years, all attention and funding has been focused on the construction of new buildings – many of which were essential for efficient agriculture, with its stated aim of national self-sufficiency in foodstuffs. Generous ministry grants, from 1957 onwards, made this spate of building possible.[1] The 'patch and mend' philosophy that had been in existence since the late Victorian agricultural slump was discarded. The farming world moved with alacrity from one extreme to the other; the enthusiastic embracing of the new in the 1960s and early 1970s could perhaps be compared in extent to the clean-sweep policy of planning in city centres operating at the same period. But there the similarity ends. On the farm, unlike the city centre, most of the older buildings still stand. Despite heavy losses, enough traditional farmsteads remain, in whole or in part, to make it essential that all the official bodies involved begin to formulate policies to help owners to retain them. Rehabilitation of housing has become commonplace; rehabilitation of farm buildings should, and is beginning to, follow. The final section of this book is concerned with that subject; the news is not all bad.

In *The Farm* I have endeavoured to sketch in something of the background to the buildings that still stand, as well as something of the foreground. The photographs, few of them known examples, make their own point. They show an astonishing diversity of buildings: vernacular or professionally designed; in good and bad states of repair; of brick or of stone; for grain or for animals; for big landowners or small hill farmers.

The brief sections on agricultural landscape and siting, as well as the one on the farmhouse (which also attempts to catch a glimpse of the men who used these buildings), are an endeavour to explain how buildings such as these came to be. I have dealt with the different types of building, and how they reflect their original functions, as well as the different agricultural practices of the various parts of England and Wales – each confusingly diverse in every respect. The nineteenth century may have standardized building materials but it could not standardize agriculture – even today the ancient divisions between the large-scale lowland mixed and arable farming and the small-scale upland pastoral agriculture remain intact.

Thirty years ago none of this would have aroused much comment; the rupture with the countryside was only just beginning. When Edwin Smith published his evocative photographs, the farmstead was still an echo of the late Victorian arrangement, often itself the product of earlier building, change and accretion.[2] Many of the farms illustrated here share the characteristics of those that Smith visited just after World War II. The wealth of fine old farm buildings that remains in the 1980s is indeed remarkable.

The Farm then is a celebration. It celebrates the fact that although amalgamation and technical advances (both necessary and unnecessary) have brought waste and redundancy, and destruction and ugliness, to the farm-yard, remarkably enough the links between traditional farming and modern agriculture are not *quite* broken, and those links are expressed in the buildings as nowhere else.

Author's note

The book divides into two sections: the first is a general appraisal of the farm and its buildings; the second is a region by region review, with the object of throwing light on the geological, economic and historical conditions which have caused the variations across England and Wales.

In order not to overburden the reader with footnotes, biographical details of the leading figures in agriculture are carried on pages 252–4.

I have divided the second part into nine regions, not all of them necessarily homogeneous in terms of agricultural practice or building styles. The source material mainly pre-dates the reorganization of the counties and the new system, therefore, is a wonderful inducement to confusion. If any errors have arisen perhaps some of the blame can be apportioned to the architects of local government reorganization?

There is no public access to most of the buildings illustrated, with the exception of tithe barns such as Great Coxwell and Frocester Court. The only farms named, therefore, are those that are already the subject of published material.

The Landscape

Right: Hill farming in the Pennines. Small enclosed fields like these are probably of 18th- or 19th-century origin. The barns provided storage for hay and shelter for animals. In some areas almost every field has such a barn, virtually all disused.

Below: East Anglian landscape near Bacton, Suffolk. Arable farming is encouraged by the low rainfall and the flat, fertile land. The field shapes combine ancient boundaries with modern scale.

Soil and terrain have dictated the patterns of agriculture from earliest times, encouraging or deterring one crop or another, one kind of livestock or another. The key to every aspect of the farm is provided by the underlying geology and the climate (itself modified by the lie of the land). For our farming ancestors, aspiring to develop a particular piece of land, be it in the Iron Age or in the Tudor period, the environment suggested the site, provided the possible building materials and then sustained the chosen form of agriculture.

The principal geographical difference governing the form of the landscape, and thus the type of farming and the nature of its buildings, is between the so-called 'upland' and 'lowland' regions of England and Wales. The distinction is surprisingly clear – the north of England, the Pennines, Wales and the south-west peninsular comprise the former category; the remainder the latter. Almost the entire upland zone lies to the west of the country – the only exception being north-east Yorkshire and parts of Northumberland.

Hill farming forms the bulk of agriculture in the upland zone and is based on livestock rearing, while arable and mixed farming dominates lowland areas. To perceive the effects of both geology and climate on agricultural patterns, contrast the flat, fertile land of Essex with Powys in mid-Wales, most of which is well over 500 ft above sea level. Essex has an annual average rainfall of less than 25 ins, whereas in Powys it is at least three times as high. There, the poor

Upland England and Wales.

The great division in agriculture
lies between upland and lowland
farming. Land over 500 to 600 ft
is generally given over to
pastoral farming.

Key

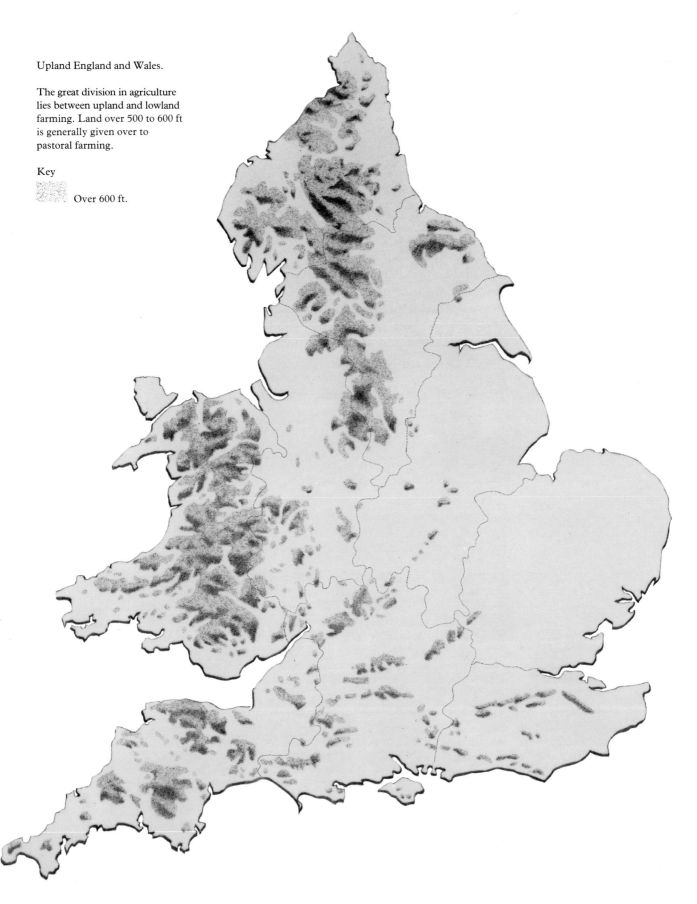

Over 600 ft.

rough moorland, and even the best land in the valleys, has dictated a pastoral economy with sheep and cattle predominating. Essex, on the other hand, has been suited to arable cultivation ever since the forests that covered it were first cleared by early farmers. Clues to this original woodland have been left in the hedges and coppices that the farmers retained to protect livestock and to provide supplies of timber for fuel, implements and construction.

Essex and mid-Wales represent two extremes of condition, but there are many intermediary shades and all are part of the same chain of circumstance. Our farming ancestors had to abide by limitations of climate, by the lessons the land conveyed in its natural vegetation, by the fact that ground at or near sea level could not produce the same crops as land at a much higher level. None of the limitations, however, has proved more insurmountable than that of climate, nor as constantly unpredictable.

In the western upland areas, high average rainfall, constant humidity and heavy, water-logged valley soils and acid hillside scrubland would support only cattle and hardy sheep. The need for self-sufficiency in the past meant the farmers had to fly in the face of these limitations and grow corn, but it was not ideal. Only the southern valleys could do so successfully. In pastoral regions the breeds might change, even the preference for dairy or beef herds, but the potential for change stops there. Climatic considerations and fertile grasslands encouraged cattle rearing in Cheshire and the plains of Lancashire. The light rainfall, drying winds and plentiful sunshine of the Yorkshire and Lincolnshire Wolds and much of East Anglia were ideal for great acreages of corn. Equally, sunshine and the absence of hard frosts made fruit- and hop-growing a speciality of the South and West.

Modern agriculture, with scientifically improved strains of seed and aids such as grain dryers and speedy processing, is much more independent of the whims of the weather. Nevertheless, out in the fields, rainfall or frost in a bad winter can still ruin a field of potatoes or sugar beet; storms and high humidity can wreck a corn crop. Farmers are still not impervious to the forces that affected their predecessors.

The landscape we see today, amidst which the buildings in the book stand, is a largely cultivated one; the result of constant incursions into new territory and of successive waves of activity. The landscape that the early farmer carved out for himself was determined by the natural conditions he encountered. Obviously he first sought to make an impression on accessible land, cleared from woodland where necessary, then on waste ground, and as demand for food grew, on progressively more intractable territory.

The landscape in the pastoral areas of Devon and Cornwall may commemorate the efforts of the Celtic farmers who, in the Iron Age, cleared small pastures for their livestock and grouped their houses into hamlets. The pattern survives, as do the massive boulders that they heaved into place as boundaries (the earliest form of enclosure) or out of which they built their rudimentary houses. The results of different farming activity over the centuries can be clearly seen in some of the field patterns of the modern landscape.

As Nigel Harvey writes, 'The shape and line of field boundaries may preserve the memory of a Roman road, the work of a medieval peasant, the plans of a Tudor landlord, an agreement between Stuart villagers, a Hanoverian Act of Parliament or the decisions of some Victorian magnate.'[1] That, neatly summarized, is the evidence of the landscape, against which the buildings, more vulnerable and prone to change and decay, are often the frail survivors of only a century or two.

By the medieval period, in the lowlands and principally in the Midland counties, a system of mixed agriculture had been established. It was carried out in great open fields, divided into a series of strips, with each man farming one or more. This 'open field' system was dependent on a crop rotation which meant that the land lay fallow for one year out of every two or three. The holdings were scattered over quite a large area and were a rather inefficient way of farming the land. Grazing was provided on common land and on fallow ground. All farm buildings lay within the village itself. The members of the village, whether closely bound to the lord of the manor or having gained a certain measure of independence, were still engaged in a basically cooperative form of agriculture with little reference to the world outside the village. Their requirement was self-sufficiency. Each, however, had a duty to his landlord – whether Church, Crown or layman – to provide him with labour or military service for allotted periods in return for the privilege of farming a portion of land. Clearly the appearance and organization of open-field agriculture had little in common with western pastoral regions or with the many districts in which men were constantly claiming farmland from moor, marsh or woodland, and settling it as independent owner-occupiers.

Following an agricultural depression in the early fourteenth century, the population was decimated by the Black Death in 1348–49, and by further outbreaks of the plague thereafter. The consequent shortage of manpower gave labour a new value, and the landless labourer came into being for the first time – an important addition to the existing pair of landowner and tenant, who had operated the open-field system between them. This new situation, along with the fluctuations of population and contortions of politics that occurred from the late fourteenth century onwards, meant that the old feudal system began to break down, and new ways of utilizing the land were sought. For example, Wilstrop, a village in the Plain of York, had twenty-eight farmhouses and cottages in the early fourteenth century. By the late fifteenth century, all trace of arable farming had gone and, despite the recorded vehement opposition from the villagers, cattle and sheep grazed a landscape of ubiquitous pasture.[2] The story was repeated across much of the lowland region – many a village lay under the thin and recent disguise of grassland. The only exception in Wilstrop was that the opposition was recorded so it could not be neatly passed off as a village where the population had been decimated by plague.

The loss of population coupled with the growth of the wool market gave the wealthy their first foot in the door towards amassing vast land holdings. It also provoked disturbance from the landless peasants, who increasingly found themselves jobless. A series of Commissions of Enquiry and several Acts of Parliament, from 1489 until 1533, were aimed at protecting, in some measure, the interests of the small man. 'The husbandry which is one of the greatest commodities of the realm, is greatly decayed,' it was observed. The 1533 Act decreed that no man might keep more than 2,400 sheep. It indicates the scale of the problem.

The agriculture that the early twentieth-century agricultural historian, Lord Ernle, described as being 'organised on principles of graduated dependence and collective responsibility' was lost. The vast sheep walks and immense holdings of the Church and the lay landlords were at the furthest extreme from the small-scale, largely pastoral agriculture practised in the ancient farmsteads of the West Country or the areas being cleared (or 'assarted', as it was also known) from the forest in the South East and elsewhere.

Ownership was to become a crucial factor in the pattern of farming and behind it the two systems of inheritance – primogeniture and partible inheritance (gavelkind). The former encouraged the building up of estates since the first born took all the land, at the expense of his brothers. Younger sons often left the land to go into the Church, the Army or into trade; eldest sons sometimes lost it through extravagance and carelessness.

Partible inheritance practised in the South East, North and West, in which the members of the family were left equal shares in a property, led to the growth of small holdings and a very different social organization, dependent on the family.[3] It probably encouraged a higher density of population, since the inducements were to stay at home, and it produced a farming pattern of small independent proprietors. Since farms in these areas were of limited acreage, they had to depend on generous commons and waste ground to provide extra grazing. As these shrank, so the practice died out, but the system of settlement endured.

Early enclosure

The processes of amassing and exchanging land are as 'ancient as farming itself.'[4] Many farms, up to the present, consist of a patchwork of scattered pieces of land, acquired piecemeal as and when the opportunity offered. The small, independent farmer of late medieval times (or much earlier, in the remoter pastoral regions) and his grandson, the Tudor yeoman, once they had built a house and farmstead, sought to increase their holdings in small ways, just as on a vastly larger scale, the great landowners did.

Enclosing and engrossing (the buying up of land wholesale), emparking and disparking (respectively, enclosing land in parks and turning park land to other uses) all have their place and specific implications in the long story of the formation of the farming landscape. The consolidation of holdings was to be greatly encouraged by economic factors. In the Elizabethan period, though agricultural methods as a whole were little changed from those of late medieval times, enclosure began to gather momentum, matching the demand brought about by the first large-scale export of produce. Goods moved from one part of the country to another, by river and sea, and they also went abroad. Corn and butter went from the West Country and Wales to Portugal, for example. Commercial incentives had awakened ideas of improving the land.

Left: Haymaking at Dixton Manor in the Severn Valley. This detail of a painting *c.* 1725–35, by an unknown artist illustrates an annual ritual. Few images of farming at such an early date exist.

Below: Harvest time, photographed *c.* 1850, at an unknown location. The fields are thickly hedged and irregular, revealing their origins as woodlands cleared for cultivation. The thatched object in the foreground would seem to be a protective clamp for vegetables.

Foreign ideas and the mounting flood of literature – although interrupted by the Civil War – were to begin to bear fruit by the post-Restoration period.

Farmers in East Anglia were growing carrots and turnips as field crops; word was coming from the Continent of further new crops and sophisticated rotation, land reclamation (in particular the Dutch expertise on the Polder) and improved fertilization. Change was in the air. It was the reorganization of land, principally through enclosure, that had made it possible.

By the time Celia Fiennes and Daniel Defoe travelled the country, in the last decade of the seventeenth century and the first decade of the eighteenth century respectively, recording their impressions, large portions of the landscape were already fully or partially enclosed. The scenes that they described were largely the small-scale enclosure efforts of independent farmers; the already well-established field patterns of much of Essex and Suffolk, Kent or Worcestershire (as well as the ancient pastures of the West Country and Wales) were taken for granted. To them could be added the more recent efforts of the new Whig ruling class, landowners whose estates were to spread vigorously into the countryside around their newly built country seats.

Field size was governed by the source of power and by the scale of farming in a particular area and at a given period. For example, until the eighteenth century, herd sizes (with the exception of hardy sheep) were limited by the difficulty the farmer found in providing fodder over a full winter period.

Other limitations on field size and shape were imposed by the energy of man and of his team of oxen or of horses. The cumbersome turning circle of a team of oxen produced a characteristic serpentine-form field, while horses, quicker but with less endurance, could be wheeled neatly more or less on the spot to give a squared-up, rectangular field. Neither animal could be forced to work beyond its capabilities and the numbers kept were limited by fodder supply.

Improved yields and new crops permitted larger herds, both of fatstock and dairy animals and of working animals. The latter provided more power, and so greater acreages could be cultivated. The population, both human and animal, was constantly rising, pushing demand for foodstuffs and fodder ahead of it.

This impetus, building up during the early eighteenth century, was to benefit the large landowner, largely at the cost of the smaller freeholder. Even the independent farmer of south-east England, his prosperous East Anglian colleague and the yeomen (or 'statesmen' as they were called in some parts) of the whole western sector of the country were losing ground in the waves of enclosure – and in the constant wish of the larger landowners to amalgamate small farms into ever larger holdings.

Parliamentary enclosure

Enclosure allowed for a sufficiently large-scale operation to give the resources, impetus and capital needed by a landowner to set about the improvement of his land, crops, stocks, implements and – always last – buildings. But the procedure was cumbersome; it might be carried out by quick mutual agreement or by protracted and embittered wrangling. It needed a proper framework and, after 1760, enclosure was increasingly carried out by Parliamentary process.

Even this caused considerable problems. François, Duc de la Roche-foucauld, travelling in East Anglia in the late eighteenth century, noticed the troubles that came because of it: 'the proprietors must be unanimous which is . . . a very difficult thing to secure'; it was also expensive and the proposer made himself unpopular. Parliamentary enclosure was, in fact, only for the landed gentry, with the necessary money and social status to carry on regardless of local feeling.

There were voices of dissent too among the experts. Nathaniel Kent, who had spent time studying farming in the Netherlands in the 1760s, and who was to become George III's bailiff for a period, addressed himself in 1775 to landed gentlemen. He lamented the loss of small farms and the 'absurd custom' of demolishing their buildings. Agriculture, he stated, 'when it is thrown into a number of hands, becomes the life of industry, the source of plenty and the fountain of riches to a country; but that monopolized, and grasped into a few hands, it must dishearten the bulk of mankind who are reduced to labour for others instead of themselves.' Kent was no tub-thumping extremist; his were the comments of the thoughtful, humanitarian man. Like the diarist parsons, Cole and Woodforde, he saw rural suffering at close hand and knew of its intensity.

The 'planned landscape' produced by Parliamentary enclosure in the eighteenth and nineteenth centuries was the product of a surveyor's carefully mapped version of the landscape, bearing in mind the controls imposed by power or possible crop acreages. Roads and even waterways were diverted, straight hedges of quickset hawthorn bordered the fields and irregularities were systematically ironed out. Even the purely ornamental park became a tree nursery or pasture land for grazing. In the past it had been deer park, game-breeding preserve or hunting ground; now, from the mid-eighteenth century onwards, it had to become part of a progressive agricultural enterprise. As the park became more utilitarian, the farmland itself became neater.

Developments in agriculture

From the 1770s onwards, the dissemination of information had become more systematic with, for example, the thorough series of Board of Agriculture reports on the state of agriculture through the counties.[5] Example now guided the farmer, not mere theory. Four-course rotation, introduced in the early eighteenth century in Norfolk, in which two corn crops alternated with sown grass, clover or roots, was widely followed by the end of the century. Such innovation constituted the movement that has subsequently become known as the Agricultural Revolution. 'Turnip' Townshend, of Raynham in Norfolk, was one of the movement's main exemplars.

The French Wars between 1793 and 1815 provided the extra impetus required to bring about the wide-scale adoption of new methods; absolutely everything had to be home-produced. The existing land had been fully exploited. New land and new methods were crucial. The seeds for improvement had been sown long ago; in these years they germinated and flourished. Hippolyte Taine, a perceptive Frenchman travelling in Britain in the 1860s, noted the clean, new look of a transformed landscape hardly a century old at most. The countryside stretching from London to York appeared to him then, as it still does today from a train or car window, 'a rectangle of greenery enclosed by a hedge, then another and so on . . .'. To a visitor from France, this was all very unfamiliar. Yet if he had visited an area further west he would have seen a landscape that had much in common with Brittany or south-west France. In upland areas, the tiny fields had been continuously and laboriously carved out of the hillsides, a 'hand-made' landscape, in W. G. Hoskins' phrase.[6] Pastoral farming, after all, had not been remodelled, nor had the landscape created by the independent farmer of the eastern or southern counties been transformed in this way.

Much land already in farming use was patently inadequate. It was water-logged and virtually useless, providing perhaps marginal grazing land. The need to extend farming land was becoming acute, in order to feed a rapidly growing urban-based population. From the late eighteenth century onwards, a massive draining enterprise began, much promoted by Arthur Young, the foremost agricultural theorist of his day, and the Board of Agriculture. After 1846, the Government made loans on tiles (clay drainage pipes) and large landowners laid them by the million. Countrywide, land previously only nominally in agricultural use became productive farm land.

Yet for all the progress there were reverses too; hard-won farmland, wrested from moor, swamp, moss or the sea, reverted to its former state both by accident and design with alarming alacrity. Much of the agricultural landscape points to such change.

The Industrial Revolution, which produced the machinery and power to cultivate more land more efficiently, also brought with it an overwhelming demand for more food production. The population was rising at an unprecedented rate but factory workers could not produce their own foodstuffs. The divide between the consumer and producer was widening all the time. The landscape everywhere had to meet those needs.

What is grown in a field today may represent centuries of constant cultivation of that crop, or a similar one. Alternatively, it may represent the triumph of man's ingenuity and technical aids over natural obstacles. It may also represent the vicissitudes of history, land ownership, demand and political events, throughout which the emphasis has shifted, for example, from corn to wool, from wool to mixed husbandry, from corn and sheep to the fattening of store livestock, from beef cattle to dairy herds and from there to wherever the Common Agricultural Policy points next. All that could, conceivably, have taken place on one lowland farm within 500 years.

The Site and Plan of the Farm

A farm at Farway, in south-east Devon, taking full advantage of a sheltered location. This farm, originally powered by a water-wheel, had 12 specialized buildings, including a cider press.

The site of the farmstead was, from the beginning, determined by water, the lie of the land and local climate. As far as the first requirement is concerned, the farmstead was usually built near a spring. Where water was not readily available, wells were dug and new ponds constructed in the fields to take advantage of any moisture and water that were available. As for climate and lie of the land, farmers who searched for sites early, as, for example, the pre-Domesday farmers of the West Country, could take advantage of a dip on a hillside which might be habitually several degrees warmer than a hill-top or valley bottom, and drier. Building types across England and Wales show careful attention to dominant characteristics of local weather.

The traditional practical dependence on the natural features of the land-scape, such as slopes or sheltered spots, meant that the suitability of the structures within the scenery was inevitable. Desperate measures to disguise modern farm buildings reflect the fact that the farmer no longer needs to seek out locations based on these considerations, but now believes access to the outside world to be his prime concern.

As farming ceased to be an exercise in self-sufficiency, so links with markets and suppliers by road, water (sea, river or canal) or railway assumed ever greater importance. Commodities had to enter or leave the farm. From the first moment that the farmer needed a supply of imported foodstuffs and chemicals, or had to depend on the professional services of a veterinary surgeon or agricultural contractor, or wanted to dispatch his milk, for example, he could not afford to be cut off. The tortuous progress of the milk tanker around the Devon lanes illustrates the conflict of ancient site with modern practice. However, most farmers work on farms in which the site has been established for many centuries and it is only the additional buildings that can be sited according to modern needs.

The siting of a farmstead is not always an accurate clue to its age or its origins, any more than are its materials – as can be seen later in this chapter. The reasons for the relationship between one farmstead and the next, or for its place within the village or outside it, are sometimes the clear result of developments in agricultural history, sometimes the accident of events. A farm of medieval origins standing alone in the fields can be the last relic of a lost village or it may have been built alone on a site chosen by an enterprising man who set about reclaiming wasteland or woodland to form an agricultural holding. Or, more commonly, an isolated farm represents a new farm, the result of post-Parliamentary enclosure reorganization.

Principal sites

There are three types of site for a farm: first, and the most ancient in origin, the farm in a smaller community, a hamlet, of which there may be several within a small radius; second, the farmstead within the nucleated village, with farms making up a considerable proportion of the buildings along the village street; third, the type mentioned above, isolated out in the fields – a product of either early clearance for agriculture or relatively recent reordering.

The farm in the hamlet is typical of upland, pastoral farming. The hamlet is also the most ancient of all sites, with Iron Age precedents. It was characteristic in areas where nucleated villages were uncommon; the cluster of two or three similar farms allowed for cooperation and mutual protection.

The farm in the village street is evidence of open-field agriculture, in which the men of the village farmed their strips of land which might be far from the site of their house and buildings. Many such villages can be found in the Midland counties, in areas such as the Isle of Axholme, the Vale of Belvoir or the Welland Valley.[1] Farmers lived close together both for protection and for convenience. Even after enclosure, the scattered pattern of some of these farms continued and to this day many farmers have holdings with patches of land spread over a large area, with little of it contiguous.

The lone farm may be the result of early clearance and settling of agricultural land or it may reflect the practices of Parliamentary enclosure. The formal brick-built two- or three-storey farmhouse, set amidst neatly enclosed fields and pastures, dates back only a couple of centuries at most – to Hanoverian or Victorian times. It is proof of the scale and breadth of the Agricultural Revolution that it should be such a standard image. The dignified form of the farmhouse and the apparent independence of the farmstead from the surrounding community (not, of course, a true picture) signified a change in stature for the farmer. Life had shifted outside the previously all-embracing envelope of the village and the fragmentation of what was once a closely-knit community, based on rural life, began then. It was the first sign of a rupture with country life which has now reached its zenith.

In much of the literature up to the early years of this century, the agricultural background is constantly brought into focus. Rogation Sunday, Plough Monday, hay making, harvest home, sheep shearing, 'largesse' (a drinking spree to mark the two latter events), and tithe dinners were focal points in the rural calendar. Tithe suppers must have been difficult, for they were an irritating imposition, even an abuse, as much for the less grasping clergy as for the farming community itself. Parson Woodforde noted the success of one such occasion in relieved tones: 'My nephew gave them a song. It was the pleasantest and most agreeable Tithe-Audit I have ever experienced. Everything harmonious and agreeable.'

The plan of the farmstead

General principles for the plan of the buildings of the farmstead were established very early. Vitruvius, the Roman architectural theorist of the first century AD, addressed himself to a similar problem and laid down some basic rules. The scale of the farmstead, he postulated, 'should depend upon the size of the farm and the amount of produce'; warmth and light were essential for the animals (it made their coats smoother – which indicated their health) and a cool well-ventilated spot should be assigned to the granary. Truths from Rome were still applicable, at least in their essentials, to the needs of the Tudor, Stuart or Hanoverian farmer.

The positioning and inter-relationship of the vernacular buildings of the farm were mainly worked out by trial and error before the eighteenth century. Wherever possible, the arrangement of buildings reflected the connection between functions, such as those between dairy and pigsty (pigs were fed from the by-products of butter- and cheese-making) or between the straw stored in the barn and the foldyard and cowshed (so that dung and straw could be mixed for the production of that farmers' 'black gold' – manure).

The scattered farmstead of the lowland counties or the more compact longhouse arrangement of the highland counties (in which convenience dictated a single roof for house, cowshed and storage of hay) served their original purpose well; however, they were not the best basis for innovative agriculture. The new agriculture required a new planned farmstead and the clean sweep made possible with the large-scale reorganization of land in the eighteenth century was ideal. But even then many farmers had to use a collection of older

Top right: A farm on the village street of Otterton, south Devon. The house is placed gable-end-on to the street while the barn lies parallel to it. The water course running alongside the street is the key to the choice of site.

Right: A farm at Blagdonburn, near Rothbury in Northumberland, sited where the enclosed fields meet the open moorland. The quickthorn hedging is typical of late 18th-, early 19th-century enclosed landscape. The stone farmhouse and buildings, neat, formal and functional, are of the same period.

buildings – it was too extravagant to destroy them. Sometimes the problem was dealt with by the development of outlying sets of buildings. A shelter shed or outlying barn saved fetching and carrying between fields and farmstead. John Worlidge, writing in the late 17th century, noted the lack of 'artificial shelters made in lands remote from our dwellings, for the speedy conveyance of corn into shelter'. In the following period the practice was widely adopted.

For animals, the housing would be sited centrally amidst the pastures, which was convenient in terms of providing manure on the spot. They usually had points of access on all sides, from the different fields. The limits of arable land determined at the time would mark the site of these outlying barns. They are an interesting record of the pushing out of limits of cultivatable land in the eighteenth and nineteenth centuries.

Even oast houses were sometimes situated out amidst the hop gardens. This decentralization of the farmyard was an important point for all advanced agriculturalists. Thomas Coke, Earl of Leicester, laid out his home farm at Holkham in Norfolk on this progressive principle, with three sets of barns (combining space for livestock with crop storage) within the park.[2] By the mid-nineteenth century James Caird, one of the foremost agricultural observers of his time, observed that in mid-Suffolk 'the occupier of a large farm prefers having several barns and feeding sheds at different points on his farm.' The introduction of portable tramway systems, making the large distances more accessible and the farmstead more flexible, together with the mobile threshing machine, made this splitting up of the farm even more feasible.

The one common factor in all farmsteads, whatever their plan, was the need for ease of access between the farmhouse and the principal buildings, usually barn and cowsheds. A yard was crucial and in many cases, especially where there was a good range of buildings, the courtyard plan had come to be accepted practice. Few Devonshire farmyards, for example, depart from this pattern. Nevertheless, as Arthur Young was to notice, most older farms consisted of 'detached straggling edifices'. Those suggesting a form for the new, planned farmstead of the Agricultural Revolution were united. William Marshall, one of the principal commentators of his day on agricultural methods, proclaimed that 'straight lines and right angles are first principles which can *seldom* be deviated from with propriety; either in laying out a farm or in planning Farm Buildings.'

The insistence on formality was to be expected; from such well-ordered surroundings would come an orderly efficient agriculture, as symptomatic of progress as the vernacular farmstead was of conservatism.

From Daniel Garrett onwards (author of the first pattern book for farmhouses, published in 1747), all farmyard plans were drawn up around a single focal point, the rectangular foldyard. It might be hollow; occasionally it was filled by a barn, sited centrally. It could be U- or E-shaped, with the open side (usually the south) allowing in the maximum amount of warmth and light. It might be multiplied into a complex affair of numerous yards, each with a purpose and related to its surrounding buildings, but the same emphasis remained – to facilitate the production and removal of manure. Arthur

Young's scorn for the 'whimsical hypothesis of those advocates of new husbandry who reject the assistance of manures' was echoed by all serious agriculturalists. The other two fixed points of every planned farmyard were the house and the principal barn. Often these two buildings were of an earlier date and the new and improved farmstead was fitted around them.

In the new view of farming, the social status of the farmer had risen; he did not want to gaze out over a sea of manure (nor did he wish to smell it) and so the new house was generally turned away from the farmyard, facing south. If the house included a servants' wing, that would lie behind. Sometimes it was shifted further still, but where the farmer's wife was liable to be the dairymaid as well it was important that she should be close to the milking sheds and pigsties. If dairy and granary were within the house, it was likely they would be on the back or north side. In John Plaw's published scheme for a northern farmhouse, the 'dairy is sunk, which in Yorkshire is considered as very advantageous'. This device kept the room quite cool, even under heat-wave conditions.

The barn, it was usually suggested, should be sited to the north; if the south

Arthur Young's plan for a small farm, from *The Farmer's Guide*, Vol. II (1770). An early example of a plan for an improved farmyard, it puts feeding racks around the perimeter of the sheep yard, and sites the straw and hay ricks close to the barns so that they can be forked directly inside. For larger farms the plan was diversified but not substantially altered.

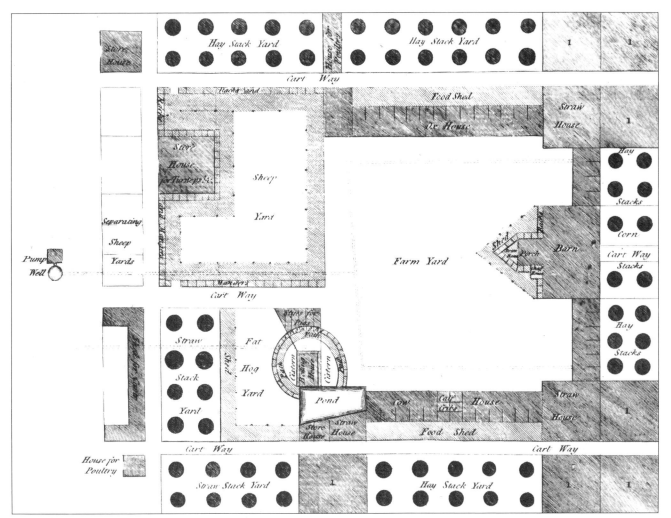

side of the yard was open, then good use could be made of sun and drying winds. Other buildings had special characteristics which affected the plan; the cart-shed should be out of the sun and, for convenience, on the outer side of the yard. Animal shelters and hay lofts, if open-fronted, needed to be in the warmest, sunniest position possible, sheltered from wind and rain. A slope helped with drainage from the livestock quarters. The placing of the farmstead as a whole was governed, as mentioned earlier, by the availability of water. If the source of water was a man-made pond, or a well or pump, then it had to be located near the livestock.

Although the relationship between cattle and straw for the manure-making process was of paramount importance, other animals, too, had their uses in this respect. It was important that stables, pigsties, even sheep-pens, if such existed, should be sited near a storage point – manure pit, midden, foldyard or whatever else had been designed for the purpose.

The introduction of mechanization

The tools of improvement had reached different levels of farming at very different times and their effect on the plan of the farmstead was not seen until some time after they had first been introduced. Some ideas proposed in the seventeenth century were not put into practice until the nineteenth. The eighteenth-century inventions of Jethro Tull, the hoe and drill, were not widely adopted for many decades after they had been invented.[3] Andrew Meikle's threshing machine, patented in 1788, was not widely enough used to be viewed as a serious threat until the 1830 machine-breaking riots, when labourers, afraid of losing their livelihood, burned barns and ricks to the ground.[4]

The farmer also faced other problems in the nineteenth century. The vicissitudes of politics were constantly providing incentives and reverses, extra demand and glut. Taxes, money supply, blockades, imports, the weather – all were for him one year, against him another.

The Industrial Revolution with its expertise in steam engines and railways provided new muscle-power in farming and the opportunity for farming to be made more efficient. An illustration of this is provided by the fact that one experienced flailman could thresh two sacks of corn per day, whereas, in the same time, a steam-driven threshing machine could fill seventy.

The formation of the Royal Agricultural Society in 1838 provided the focus for information on new methods and improvements through its publications and sponsorship. Increasing population was the driving force. By the 1840s, 'high farming', as the new mechanized agriculture came to be known, was in full swing.

In some respects the Hanoverian farmstead proved quite adaptable to some of the changes made necessary in the mid-nineteenth century. Covered cattle sheds had become essential equipment by this time and it proved quite easy to roof over the hollow centre of the foldyard to provide the new accommodation. The essential requirement for a courtyard-shaped farmyard remained, however much complexity might be introduced within it. New 'model' farms all took on board the Hanoverian plan and merely elaborated it to contain the advances of the intervening thirty to fifty years.[5]

The main change in the farmstead needed for 'high farming' (which was, on the whole, purpose-built from scratch) was one of scale. Engine house and threshing equipment modified the plan. Stackyards multiplied and moved further out, encouraged by mobile threshing machines. Everything could spread, since on the mechanized farm – and there was a surprising number – tramlines and conveyor belts (powered by steam) reduced the amount of labour. Fetching and carrying between, say, cattle sheds and steaming house (where root crops were processed) or root shed, became a faster business, less wasteful of man-hours.

Not only did the mechanized farmstead spread outwards but everything became larger, except the barn, which became smaller since the threshing machine had rendered it largely redundant. Yards multiplied and the range of buildings increased. Cattle sheds which used tramline track feeding systems, like that at Lord Armstrong's hydraulically powered home farm at Cragside in Northumberland, were of an immense length and thus far larger herds could be dealt with. Mobility even spread into the fields; one method of folding the ground was described by Caird. The sheep were put into slatted trolleys and trundled out on rails over the cropped fields; however, this, together with many of the more far-fetched farming aids of an age dazzled by the possibilities of power, was a short-lived solution.[6] Sheep were soon back on their feet.

In the late 1870s agriculture suffered a series of grave setbacks from which it never fully recovered until after World War II. The combination of a succession of climatically disastrous seasons and the flood of cheap imported grain coming from the developing (and mechanized) prairies of Canada, or the great Australian farmlands, left the British farmer reeling. Worst hit were arable farmers, most of whom were concentrated in the eastern counties.

In many cases gross returns on arable land fell by half their former value. The large landowner was best placed to withstand the depression; he at least had other resources. In many cases the landlord buttressed a good tenant from the most severe effects – holding down his rent and helping him to diversify into less vulnerable areas. The Royal Commission set up to investigate the agricultural depression reported, in 1882, that the small farmer was the chief victim, although, in the West Country, land that could be put into pasture for grazing is an 'easy and conservative business compared to the management of ploughland'.[7] Even there, however, the position was precarious. Chilled and frozen meat was soon appearing from those same colonial sources. Only dairying was inviolable.

It was hardly surprising that the farmstead ceased to expand or develop. Existing buildings were patched and many more fell out of use. In the early twentieth century, the landowner's function as an avenue for the introduction of the new was diminishing. Hard hit by the reverses of the late nineteenth century, he permitted this role to be taken over by the Government-run research stations. Today it might be said that the Agricultural Development and Advice Service (ADAS) is the Arthur Young of our time.

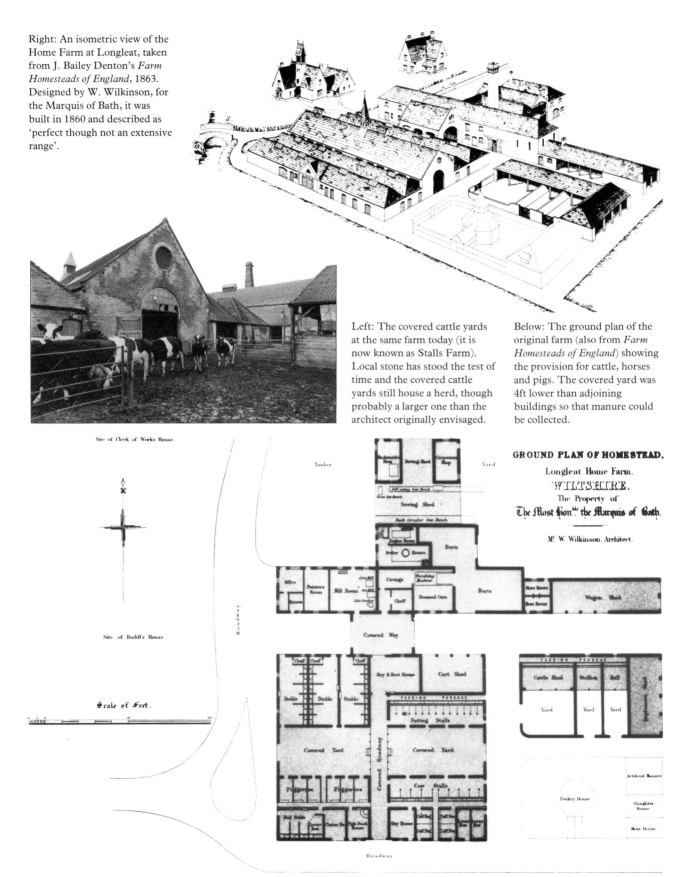

Right: An isometric view of the Home Farm at Longleat, taken from J. Bailey Denton's *Farm Homesteads of England*, 1863. Designed by W. Wilkinson, for the Marquis of Bath, it was built in 1860 and described as 'perfect though not an extensive range'.

Left: The covered cattle yards at the same farm today (it is now known as Stalls Farm). Local stone has stood the test of time and the covered cattle yards still house a herd, though probably a larger one than the architect originally envisaged.

Below: The ground plan of the original farm (also from *Farm Homesteads of England*) showing the provision for cattle, horses and pigs. The covered yard was 4ft lower than adjoining buildings so that manure could be collected.

The inter-war and modern farm

The new farmstead developed after World War I was a rarity; it tended to be a rich man's plaything, and usually took the form of an elaborate home farm. Dairying was the one area of agriculture in which expansion was possible. Herds grew larger and cow sheds of much improved design (rather than the converted cattle shed of former years) formed the centrepiece of the farmstead of the 1920s or 1930s. A handful of such schemes were generally architect-designed, in an elegant rustic style; thatched as at Rushbrooke, in Suffolk, or as at the extraordinary Node Dairy at Codicote in Hertfordshire, or built in a combination of high quality traditional materials (brick, tiling, weather-boarding) as at Barrington in Somerset.[8]

Planning of the modern farmstead has, and, in the near future, may have a very different complexion. There are signs of new ideas. Methane digesters, producing bio-gas from manure, are appearing here and there amidst the more conventional farm buildings. One Kent farm runs an elaborately designed 300-cow milking unit on the power the cow dung produces. However, the concern still remains in the area of design. Despite various attempts to alert the farmer and landowner to the virtues of careful siting and proper design, and despite the design manuals produced regionally and nationally to cajole the farmer into choosing fitting colours, finishes and forms, little improvement can be seen in the landscape as a whole. Massive regiments of sheds, bought from a catalogue as ready-made units, are the functional containers of the new large-scale agriculture in which bulk reigns supreme (larger herds, more grain, larger combine harvesters). Often, they encircle the core of older buildings on the farm (used more widely and to better effect than might at first sight appear to be the case). Aesthetics have never had much to do with farming, since practicality and utility have always been the central considerations. Perhaps good husbandry and good advice under the present constrained economic conditions will give a place to the best of the new, as of the old.

Barrington Court, Somerset – a contemporary photograph of an exceptionally fine farm of the 1920s, designed by Forbes and Tait. The sequence of barns and cattle sheds on the right is of stone, concrete and elm boards. The hipped gables disguise the hoists to the lofts. The buildings line the road from the farmhouse (out of picture) to the agent's house in the distance. The farm remains unchanged today.

Materials and Construction

Above: The tithe barn at Pilton in Somerset, built for an Abbot of Glastonbury. The quatrefoil serves as decoration, ventilation and an entry-exit for owls.

Below: Magpie farmer, Sledmere, north Humberside.

Like the site itself, materials are clues to evolution and history on the traditional farmstead. But the evidence can be misleading. Many a farm building has been put together out of the fragments of an earlier building, perhaps with the date-stone reinstated over the door as an unintentional red herring. In particular, after the Dissolution of the Monasteries in the mid-sixteenth century, innumerable religious buildings fell into agricultural use; chapels became barns and dormitories were turned into cattle sheds. Often the name of the farm, 'Priory', 'Chapel' or 'Abbey', is a clue to its former use, while a fragment of arcading, a cusped window detail or a fluted door jamb provides the physical evidence.

The farmer has always been a magpie, with an eye for adaptation and expedient re-use, a skill as unerring in the sixteenth century as it is today, when an old railway carriage or a tin bath finds some useful purpose around the place. Even the solemn theorists of the Hanoverian planned farmstead thought there should be no waste; Robert Beatson advocated the re-use of materials since they were cheap and to hand. However, he added a cautionary note that workmen, especially carpenters, did not like using second-hand materials.

The best materials were those provided by the ground underfoot. We know that the medieval farmers used mud and split shavings of timber, or twigs, for their buildings; but it comes as a surprise to find Plaw in the late eighteenth century advocating *pisé* (mud brick) in the face of competition from brick (by then both locally made and imported by canal) or stone. Thatching, which many advanced thinkers at that time had decided was an outmoded material, was still also being advised, sometimes because of its self-consciously rustic look – people were already looking to the countryside to supply an image of rustic prettiness. The twentieth century cannot claim a monopoly on the liking for contrived charm.

Of course, the materials of farm buildings have in the past served their purpose excellently. The ventilation afforded by wattle or weather-boarding, or by the simple expedient of leaving out a brick or a stone or two (and sometimes making a virtue out of necessity, and forming a pattern in this way), has no modern substitute. As in clothing, natural materials can usually beat the new man-made substitutes and many traditional features have subsequently been included in professionally designed structures.

Variations in these features appear within a small area, indications of the complexity of the geology that guides the choice of material. Until the nineteenth century, the buildings of an area reflected with absolute clarity these local changes (the only exceptions being in those grander buildings that justified the import of materials, brick into a stone area, stone into a timber area and so on). Thus on the finger of the Suffolk–Norfolk border known as Breckland, where poor, sandy topsoil overlays chalk, the dominant building material is flint, edged with bricks made from nearby clays. Just a few miles away the geological change is immediately obvious; the older farmhouses are timber-framed, the panels infilled with lath and plaster, telling of wooded valleys and oak forests long gone. Traditionally, as materials were handled in a predominantly functional way, only a tiny decorative flourish, such as the

Geology of England and Wales. The building materials used prior to the Industrial Revolution were largely dependent on the underlying geology of the area. The map, right, shows the principal rock and soil formations of England and Wales. During the period when timber was a widely used building material much of the country was heavily wooded, the best timber growing on the rich clay soils.

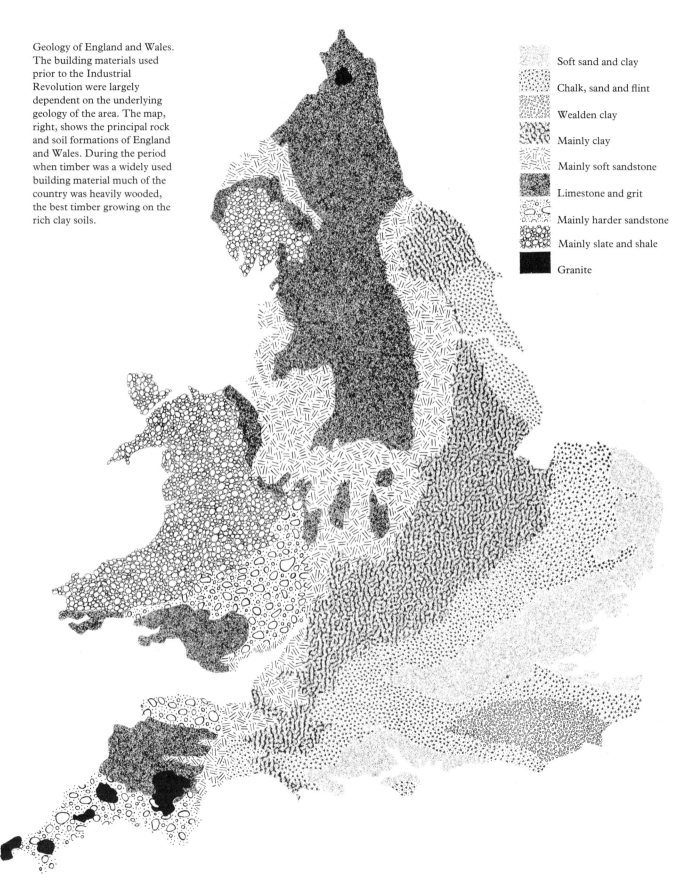

Soft sand and clay

Chalk, sand and flint

Wealden clay

Mainly clay

Mainly soft sandstone

Limestone and grit

Mainly harder sandstone

Mainly slate and shale

Granite

31

forming of patterns with the ventilation spaces, could be justified. However, much as the landowner or agent might like to flex his muscles as an architectural patron, and follow the fashion, there was no agricultural reason for neoclassical trimmings, battlements or polychrome bricks. Nevertheless, the medieval carpenter had set the precedent for a touch of style, and the introduction of a little non-utilitarian decoration. When times were good, such extravagance could be condoned. When economy was of the essence, they were quickly set aside.

Timber-framing

Timber is, of course, the one material that has been an ubiquitous element in the buildings of the farmstead – from the days of the yeoman farmhouse and its outbuildings to a modern shed of Yorkshire boarding (widely-spaced slatting). The art of carpentry had reached astonishing sophistication in the great barns of the medieval period, erected to receive tithes in kind. Equally, the remarkable survival of many hundreds of humbler barns and houses of the late medieval and Tudor periods attests to the quality of the materials used and the expertise in construction.

The discussion of the variations of timber-framing is a complex, specialist subject making any simplification misleading.[1] A number of basic external frame types have been identified, with regional and chronological variations. The subtler processes of development can be gauged by the evolution of the roof structure and the way in which the principal posts are set into the ground. Where the building is found to rest on a system of sills rather than being planted directly into the earth, there is an indication that the building was expressly designed so that it could be moved.

In both barns and farmhouses, cruck and box frames are the two principal

Right: A simple 8-bay timber-framed barn, designed for Wimple Hall, Cambridgeshire, by Sir John Soane in 1794. The barn still stands at Park Farm. It is thatched and has later additions and is incorporated within a quadrangle of farm buildings. A standard threshing barn, with two entries on the south side, it was designed within the carpentry traditions of the period and region, with which Soane was well familiar.

Left: Farms grouped into hamlets at Hartsop, Cumbria – a typical pattern in pastoral agriculture, found also in western England and in Wales, and in western France.

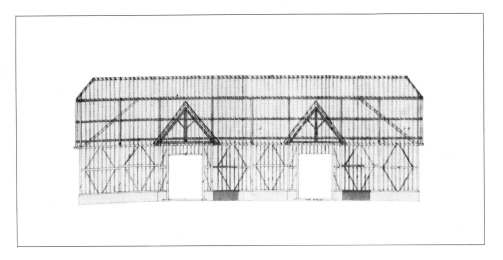

categories, modified internally by their division of space and roof trusses into innumerable variations – all proof of date and history to the trained eye. The latter point is important, bearing in mind that so many barns have probably been reconstructed on a different site, or modified as they stand. Adaptability and mobility were great advantages of the system. The aisled form of plan and the hammer-beam roof construction are two of the most impressive variants.[2]

The cruck frame is found virtually over all the country except in the south and south east of England. It consists of a series of spaced pairs of matching timbers, often split from the same trunk, each pair meeting in an inverted 'V'. The spaces between each pair of timbers along the length of the construction are known as bays. The structure is strengthened along its length with ties. The form, like a kind of tea cosy, allows the outer skin to be almost free-standing. In many northern areas, a cruck frame is hidden beneath the disguise of a stone exterior. The cruck frame was superseded by a variation, known as the post and truss system, which preserved the bay system of the cruck frame within the basic construction of the box frame.

Although the cruck frame was constructed in remoter areas as late as the eighteenth century, it was generally demoted by then, being used for barns and outbuildings rather than for housing.

The box structure, perfected in those areas in which the cruck was never developed, consists of separate roof timbers resting on a series of sturdy principal posts and horizontal members. The wall panels would be variously filled with, for grander examples, a filigree of timbering or with thin studs, exposed vertical timbers, infilled with wattle and daub (mud), lath and plaster, brick or even stone (sometimes plastered over). The sets of important horizontal and vertical timbers are constrained by internal tie beams to prevent the shell of the box springing out. The studs are spaced further apart in western areas, while in eastern England they are closely spaced. With the box frame, a jetty, or overhanging upper storey, was possible. Though developed first to take advantage of limited space in towns, the jetty became a distinctive feature in farmhouses, from the Wealden house to the splendid examples of the West Midland counties.

Right: The hammer-beam roof of a manorial barn at Winterbourne Clenston in Dorset. The roof timbers of 15th-century date were taken from a monastic building. The barn itself is probably late 16th-century. Clunch and brick walls support the seven hammer-beam trusses.

Below: Cruck barn at Hacking Hall, Billington, north Lancashire. Stone walls, modern roofing and an extension at the end do little to suggest the magnificence of the interior. Now a cattle shed, the barn would formerly have been used as a hay store.

Opposite: A 17th-century cruck barn near Barlow in Derbyshire. The barn has four pairs of crucks and is clad with stone.

The longest completely roofed barn in the country, stretching 210 ft, at Frindsbury, Kent. It dates from the early 14th century, or possibly even earlier. The building is of aisled construction and the roof is supported on 12 king posts. Here the aisles are seen used for the storage of baled straw.

Choice of materials

With regard to the choice of wood in Elizabethan England, the contemporary historian Harrison states: 'In times past men were contented to dwell in houses built of sallow, willow, plum tree, hardbeam [hornbeam] and elm . . . but now all these are rejected, and nothing but oak any whit regarded.' By the time of Marshall's reports 200 years later, oak had become scarce and phenomenally expensive; imported woods had already begun to find uses. Woodland had been enormously depleted and, for hop poles, fencing, implements and constructional purposes of the farm, the still luxuriant hedges often provided the raw materials. For the less important functions that wood had, on the whole, now been relegated to perform, in the shape of hidden roof timbers or boarded floors, the quality was less important. Carpentry skills were, in any case, dying out and the softwood timber-framed buildings of the late eighteenth and nineteenth centuries were structures much inferior to their predecessors. For infilling of walls, wattle was elaborate to construct and tended to be nibbled by animals, and for wall construction, lath and plaster required, similarly, both skill and time; stone or brick generally took their place. In another half century, farm buildings would be transformed with the introduction of iron, which could significantly increase the span of a building, without the need for cumbersome supports. Cast-iron would be used for columns in shelter sheds, for tie-rods across the width of barns, and was ideal for guttering and downpipes, which greatly increased the chances of survival for older buildings with faulty roofs.

The choice of materials and finishes was used to confer importance on the various buildings round the farmstead. Brick, stone, slates or tiles brought from a distance would inevitably be more expensive. Engravings of the great houses, grandiose barns and stables for working horses in the late seventeenth and early eighteenth century, showed many of the buildings of the home or park farm at that period; the grand barns and stables (the latter often with glazed windows, apparently made habitable for the labourers) contrast strongly in form and in the use of materials with the meaner sheds which matched the cottages nearby in their rudimentary styles.[3] Carriage horses were accorded superior architectural forms. Their stables were often built by the architect of the great house in scarcely less grand manner.

Similar gestures were traditionally made by the vernacular builder to distinguish the house from farm buildings often attached to it; in Kent, the roof and walls of the house would be tiled and tile-hung and the outbuildings thatched; in Cumbria, whitewash extended only to the domestic quarters. Wordsworth noticed the distinction, and it still applies.

In the eighteenth and early nineteenth century, such was the vogue for the box-like, four-square farmhouse (as opposed to its often gabled and certainly irregular predecessor) that many a rambling, asymmetrical sixteenth- or seventeenth-century house was fronted with a skin of brick or stone in the new mode. Only the layout of the rooms inside (and sometimes the older materials exposed round the back) gave such disguises away. Thus, although the buildings of the farmstead were principally concerned with the essentials, a measure of licence was allowed where the public face was concerned.

Left: A Hertfordshire coppice, a reminder of the farmer's former dependency on timber to provide shelter, fencing posts, chips for wattle and laths as well as fuel.

Below: Yorkshire boarding for modern cattle sheds. Wooden buildings, unlike asbestos ones, allow for ventilation.

Above: Cut-and-laid hedging in Buckinghamshire. A rare survival of a rural craft with a practical use, making hedges animal-proof and encouraging dense growth.

Left: Timber-framed barn with wattle panels at Frampton-on-Severn in Gloucestershire. Walls constructed from panels of interlaced wood shavings or wattle provided good ventilation. To prevent cattle nibbling it, the wattle started high up.

In upland areas the traditionally built farmhouse, outbuildings and walling are all of stone. The boundaries, sometimes built up with materials from older buildings long gone, snake over the Pennine hills, bravely trying to keep back the moor. Many of these characteristic dry-stone walls are of comparatively recent date, contemporary with the neat hedges of quickthorn planted by eighteenth-century landowners under Parliamentary enclosure.

Right: Dry-stone walling near Elkstone in the Cotswolds. The builder has skilfully selected random shapes of stone to make a neat, secure wall.

Below: Walling near Crawford, in north Devon – the hedge on top gives a dense protection to the field edges in an uncertain climate of much wind and rain.

Below right: Walling and steps in Swaledale, North Yorkshire.

Above left: Slivers of granite and slate used to key in the windows on a farm building at Kentmere Hall, Cumbria. Although the upper window is now blocked up, its position is still clearly marked.

Above: Local slate and heavier gritstone used for walling in farm buildings at Mathafarn, Machynlleth, Wales.

Left: Walling on a farm at Withnell in Lancashire – note the tethering ring for a farm horse or pony.

The characteristics of local brick depended on the type of clay and methods of firing it in the region. Similarly, the wide variations of stone within a small area were dictated by local geology though, in general, upland areas yield a hard stone, the lowlands softer, sedimentary ones. Construction methods and local traditions of brick-laying and masonry further varied the type of finish to be found; in stone areas, the finished effect could be anything from a rough-looking random rubble surface to the elegance of coursed ashlar – reserved for house, dovecote and principal barn, and perhaps as a trim for other buildings. Some areas had their own mixtures of material (mentioned in the appropriate regional sections) giving rise to the rich patterns, textures and colours of materials such as colour-washed cob, clay bat, clunch, plaster, rough-cast or pebble-dashed rendering and flints. As time went on, the mixtures became more adventurous: nineteenth-century farm buildings in central Oxfordshire, for example, are of stone, with brick quoins and door and window surrounds. Some Wiltshire farm buildings incorporate almost innumerable types of material – a kind of layer-cake of available geological specimens. However, by the late eighteenth century and early nineteenth century the local variations were fading out. Standardized materials were coming in by canal and railway to replace those of the immediate locality. Technical advances had made them cheaper; quarrying and brick-making on a small scale were expensive and, on the whole, could ill compete with mechanized concerns. The farm buildings of the Hanoverian and Victorian period present us with a more or less uniform image from Staffordshire to Essex, from Devonshire to Lincolnshire. The homogeneity of materials echoed the standardization of plans.

A typical piece of mid-19th-century ironwork from Essex.

Left: 19th-century flint and brick walling, Winfrith Newburgh, Dorset.

Below left: High-quality brickwork on an 18th-century barn at Sledmere, Humberside. The circular 'window' is a pitching hole.

Above: A random pattern of hand-made Norfolk bricks.

Below: Pierced 19th-century brickwork on a barn at Moston, near Sandbach, Cheshire. Ventilation is provided by omitting the header at every third brick.

Where roofing was concerned, there had always been abundant materials at hand. Heather, bracken or even bundles of twigs were used, as well as the more obvious straw or reed thatch. In some cases wooden shingles were used instead. The finish, and the flourishes of the thatcher, were also indicative of the importance of the building, although the straw-rick, only there for the season, was nevertheless given a careful and expert casing as well. However, thatching was to be gradually given up, as tiles (themselves of many types, forms and colours) took its place. They had the advantage of providing better ventilation (on some buildings they were spaced quite widely apart) as well as better protection. Slates and stone tiles were to replace thatch in areas where they were easily obtained, such as, respectively, Wales or the Cotswolds.

When the pattern book authors turned their attentions to the use of materials – theorizing somewhat after the event – they produced some elegant justifications. Nathaniel Kent, writing in the 1780s, advised that barns should be thatched in case the labourers pushed their pitchfork prongs through while piling up straw; also because tiles could be dangerous in windy conditions. He also offered some hints on wood. As good timber became scarcer and more expensive, cheap weather-boarding was advised – it could be made from inferior wood and from the lesser limbs of the tree.

When it came to detail, the available materials proved adaptable. Slatted windows and doors, louvred ventilators and improvised partitions could be made up out of odd cuts of wood. Pitching holes or 'eyes' could easily be inserted into the stone or brickwork. Racks and troughs could be made of wood and built up with slate, stone or brick, if necessary. Floors could be of board, or they could be flagged or cobbled. All this developed by trial and error. Only when modern legislation, aimed at hygiene and the eradication of prevalent livestock diseases, came into force did uniformity of detail arrive – the concrete floors of the cow sheds are one such example.

Factory-made buildings

The fittings and fabric of the late Victorian farmstead were factory-made in their entirety. Bricks, tiles, guttering, equipment, all came by train from a factory – ordered from the catalogue or bought from a supplier. Nowadays the modern farm building often comes complete; concrete breeze blocks and metal sheeting, asbestos and lightweight boarding have replaced even Gertrude Jekyll's hated corrugated iron (which we, contrarily, begin to grow fond of).[4] The new shed probably has been sold complete by a manufacturer – off-the-peg, like the feeding racks that the Victorians bought by catalogue description.

There could hardly be a stronger contrast to the patched-up old farmstead – its materials found locally and its forms and colours fitting predictably into the surrounding landscape. Now the sheds are green, or blue, or whatever colour has been suggested most recently as 'inoffensive'. There are a few fine modern farm buildings – but so far regrettably not enough. Sometimes the bravest are the best, such as the steel-panelled grainstores that can be seen dotted around Essex. Confidence is rare in new architecture and rarer still on the farm.

Above, far left: Slate tiles used for Cornish foldyards and shelters, Roscarrock.

Above, left: Thatching on a barn at Shalbourne, Wiltshire.

Far left: Pantiles and brick at Blickling, Norfolk. These ridged tiles are found all over the East Coast of England; they were originally imported from Holland.

Left: Timber cowl and weathervane at Shalbourne, the cowl acting as a ventilation duct for a kiln below.

The Farmhouse

The one place where, at least until the Victorian age, all the activities and the people of the farm met, was in the farmhouse. Through its development, we can follow the increasingly specialist function of each room or part of the house.

The medieval hall house

The late medieval farmhouse, a hall house, is the first type for which there is any substantial built evidence or any written records. Here the main concern was to divide the space simply between the main hall or living area and the service rooms, in particular those required for storage and preparation of food and drink. In the upland regions, where the buildings were generally smaller, the space was even more simply divided between the main hall and the area used for animal shelter.

A Suffolk moated farmhouse built around 1450 at Haughley, near Stowmarket, from the profits made by a merchant who smuggled wool out of the country and brought silk in. The house was added to in the Tudor period to provide more accommodation.

Right: A good example of a Wealden house, box-framed and close-studded. It has a recessed centre bay and two jettied bays flanking it. It was built at Bletchingley in Surrey in the 15th century.

Late 19th-century photograph of a farm at Eardisley in Herefordshire, seen from the north side. The farmhouse disguises a core from the mid-15th century. The medieval hall house had an open hall, passage and solar (parlour), the latter to the north. In the late 16th century, early 17th century, the hall was floored over, chimneys were added and large new extensions were built. To the west were family rooms, to the east, where the catslide roof runs down over the outshut, were the dairy, scullery, kitchen and other service areas. The house, with its midden and later farm buildings, is an excellent example of the development of the farmhouse for the Tudor yeoman's needs, with its demarcation between domestic and service quarters within the house.

The hall, the single principal space in the house, whatever its size, spanned the height from floor to ceiling. It would either be on the ground floor, with aisles, or slightly raised above a storage area and reached by steps. Off this main room would be one smaller room, a chamber, in which the family slept. The farm labourers would sleep in the hall or, more usually, with the animals in outbuildings. There might be a buttery for the storage of drink and a pantry for food and a detached kitchen. These rooms, representing the essential needs of the farmer, his family and if necessary any employees, were fitted together in various ways. As M. W. Barley says, they formed a 'catalogue of pieces which were, in one region or another, arranged in various combinations'.

Windows were vestigial, the openings shuttered or covered by oiled paper or horn, with the smoke from the fire escaping via the gablet, a small aperture in the inverted 'V' of a hipped roof, a feature borrowed by the barn for ventilation. Another feature shared with the barn was the threshold, which in the house was the dividing cross-passage between the living and the service rooms, and in the barn the threshing floor.

The Wealden house

It was in the south east of England, from the late fourteenth century onwards, that innovation in the construction of the farmhouse first appeared, partly as a result of it being a wealthy district with many family-owned farms, the product of the laws of partible inheritance. It took the form of the Wealden house – a more sophisticated version of the hall house, sometimes with two living rooms and two service rooms, separated by a cross-passage. The lower chamber, which became known as the parlour, was floored over and the upper chamber was reached by a simple staircase or ladder. Although it was originally the store place for wool, apples or grain, it was to become the main sleeping room of the developed Wealden house. This type of house also had the rudiments of two wings at either end of the house in the form of jettied, or overhanging, bays. The Wealden plan eventually spread far outside the limited corner of Kent and Sussex from which it drew its name. The affluent Kentish yeoman farmer of the fifteenth century was living in conditions far in advance of his counterpart in the Midlands, for example.

The longhouse

The small farmer of remote pastoral regions and rougher upland areas was furthest from these influences. There the longhouse, like its more developed eighteenth-century descendant, the laithe-house, combined the housing of the farmer and his livestock, together with the storage of all their goods and fodder, under one roof. The arrangement was advantageous, particularly in a wet climate and in dairying areas where constant attention had to be given to the cattle all the year round.

The two functions were partitioned from one another, at least from Tudor times. The division was usually in the form of a cross-passage, from either side of which access could be gained to the living space of the farmer, or that of his animals. Later development led to the complete separation of the two areas, the only link being in their shared roof. The longhouse was single-storeyed

Above right: A Wealden farmhouse near Edenbridge, Kent. It has Kentish framing (arc-shaped timbers) and a hipped roof. Unlike a classic Wealden house, it is not jettied at the front, merely at the sides; nor does it have a central recessed bay. A drawing of 1881 shows the dormer window already inserted.

Right: Well-wooded landscape near Shipley in the Sussex Weald, with weather-boarded field barns.

Overleaf: Glencoyne, a 'statesman's' farm at Patterdale in Cumbria. The farmhouse and barn-cum-cow byre (or shippon) are joined together in typical longhouse fashion. The front door opens onto a cross-passage leading to the back door. The cylindrical chimneys and crow-stepped gables are characteristic of buildings in this area, and the house has a 1629 datestone.

Above: The cross-passage in an ancient cob and thatch farmhouse near Chagford, north Devon.

Left: The timber frame, *c.* 1560, of Chorley Old Hall, Alderley, Cheshire, disguises one of the most ancient surviving hall houses of its type, dating from the mid-14th century. It consisted of a hall and two-storey solar wing: the house was surrounded by a moat. Unlike other surviving houses from this period, it was an early version of a yeoman farmhouse, not a manor. The earliest farm buildings extant date from the mid-17th century, and are outside the moat, to the north.

with the domestic accommodation divided, as in the lowland farmhouse, between living and sleeping space. Harrison noticed that the placing of 'stable and all offices under one roof . . . is to be seen in the fenny countries and northern parts.' He compared it with the practice in richer lowland areas where the farm was

> builded in such sort generally as that they have neither dairy, stable, nor brew-house annexed unto them under the same roof (as in many places beyond the sea and some of the north parts of our country), but all separate from the first, and one of them distant from another.

However, in many areas of pastoral agriculture, such as in the West Country, both upland- and lowland-type farmhouses could be found.

The Tudor yeoman and his house

The yeoman farmer, characterized by Trevelyan as one of the categories of a new 'middle class' – with squires, lawyers and merchants – was a particular character. These farmers were, in his words, 'men of the new age, not hankering after feudal ideals now passing away . . . they evolved a kind of religion of the home, essentially "middle-class" and quite unmedieval'.

From Lambarde we receive an idyllic portrait of the Kentish yeoman farmer: 'in manner every man is a freeholder, and has some part of his own to live upon. And in this their estate, they please themselves, and joy exceedingly . . . nor desire to be apparelled with the titles of gentry.' His Devon counterpart

> gives himself for the most part to such virtues, conditions and qualities as does the gentleman, and delights in good housekeeping, fares well, seemly in his apparel, courteous in his behaviour, and friendly to his neighbours . . . his chief travails be most in matters of his husbandry wherein he leaves no pains to make his best profit, whether it be by tilling, grassing, buying and selling of cattle. [1]

The houses of these men, independent freeholders or at least customary (that is, secure) tenants, expressed a reassuringly recognizable change in style.

The development of the farmhouse has to be understood in terms of the needs and the status of its occupants. The 1570s saw the stirrings of a major building boom, the 'Great Rebuilding', which lasted until the Civil War. As Harrison put it,

> every man almost is a builder, and he that hath bought any small parcel of ground, be it never so little, will not be quiet till he have pulled down the old house (if any there were standing) and set up a new after his own device.

Despite his words, no doubt true of his own wealthy county of Essex, many farmers were content to keep their medieval hall house but added to it a service wing, even two, and roofed over the hall itself to gain overhead sleeping accommodation, and possible storage space as well. It was a practical notion, for the warmth from the fire below was trapped in the smaller upper spaces.

The cross-passage, too, became more elegant, often formed from panelled wood, earning it the name of screens passage. In Barley's words, 'the only source of the Tudor farmer's concept of an ideal home was the medieval manor house;' it was in the grander houses of the countryside that the idea of full-scale service wings had been introduced.

Farmhouses were often worth adaptation, rather than replacement, because of the excellent materials with which they had been built. Harrison noticed that, of the timbers available, only oak would do for house building in the late sixteenth century; nevertheless, 'such as are lately builded are commonly either of brick or hard stone, or both.' These superior (and often expensive) materials defined the farmhouse, and perhaps the principal barn and stables, as the important buildings of the farmstead. Any other buildings were likely to be constructed from inferior materials – cheap and to hand – which have long since disintegrated.

Anywhere near the Continent, the new ideas gained ground with ease, influence from abroad being a spur to improvement and helping to set high standards of craftsmanship.

The new, more elaborate plan and the superior finish and materials pointed to the status of the Tudor yeoman farmer. In the new stone-built houses, there were chimneys, often serving two hearths, and thus giving a central axis; windows were larger, and glazed. Interiors, too, gave witness to increasing wealth and new aspirations. Harrison says, 'many farmers have, for the most part, learned to garnish their cupboards with plate, their joined beds with tapestry and silk hangings and their tables with carpets and fine napery.' Even in the far northern regions, there were aspirants to this style of living; the

Opposite, above: The service end of a Welsh longhouse at Llanerch y Cawr in the Elan Valley. The house was built of huge stones and cruck trusses; a door connected the domestic quarters to the cattle byre.

Opposite, below: A laithe-house at Oxnop, in north Yorkshire. The house, barn and byre share the same roof but are not connected internally and have separate entrances. The barn to the right has probably been heightened at a later date.

Below: A Dartmoor farmhouse, Lower Uppercott, photographed in 1950. The tiled outshut, which faces north, probably contained dairy and pantry.

Lakeland 'statesman' (a word derived from 'estate') was a prosperous independent farmer, still in evidence as late as the nineteenth century, according to some observers.[2] His housing was always well in the van of fashionable development, although it also had marked regional characteristics, mostly developed to deal with a very harsh climate.

The Tudor farmer, if he was sharing in the new prosperity, might live, as we have seen, in a newly built house or in an older farmhouse, converted and extended to new standards. If he remained a tenant he might also find himself living in the manor house. The larger manor house, itself an advanced and expensive version of the medieval hall house, had probably been little used over the preceding century or more; the ecclesiastical or lay landlord had perhaps visited it once or twice a year as he surveyed his properties. By the time of the Great Rebuilding many such houses had become farmhouses tenanted by working farmers. With proportions far in excess of the needs of their occupants they were falling on hard times and were often in bad repair.

In larger houses, the household's wing was divided from the service one, as in Gervase Markham's house for the rich husbandmen (to be distinguished from the 'generall Husbandman' who must 'take such a house as he can conveniently get'). The service wing had a cellar, buttery, kitchen, milkhouse and dairy-house on the ground floor and a second storey with 'goodman's rooms'. This was the provision expected in a sizeable modern farmhouse.

As some rooms moved into the house, others moved out; now that servants were more likely to be housed indoors (rather than in the wretched premises over cowsheds or stables, or in roughly converted farm buildings) they were given their own kitchen. This was a significant alteration – it signalled a social gulf, the beginning of a stratification between employer and different grades of employee; farmer and farm labourer no longer ate together. Later on still, when the labourers were shifted into the house of the bailiff or steward, it seemed more appropriate that *his* wife should cook and clean for them than the farmer's servants or family.

The back kitchen often took the place of the wash- and bake-houses and these moved into a separate structure out in the yard, as the kitchen had once been in the larger medieval house.

The dwelling of the yeoman farmer, once developed into this sophisticated form, changed little over a long period. In Dorset, for example, it is almost impossible to guess at the dates of farmhouses between the late sixteenth century and the late seventeenth century: once the type of accommodation had been arrived at and the use and treatment determined, the basic pattern was set and little changed.

Further developments
During the seventeenth century, both before the Civil War and after, when building began again, the farmhouse developed larger cross-wings, gabled porches and outshuts, a form of lean-to. The screens passage had become a lobby – the 'hall' of later terminology. In the late seventeenth century, the same influence that was affecting the design of the major country houses, that of Continental classicism, began to touch the smaller house. By then the

Top left: A large 17th-century farmhouse at Bressingham, Norfolk, built of clay bat, with a stepped gable.

Top right: Late 17th-century farmhouse at Rainford, Ormskirk, on the Lancashire/Cheshire borders. The mullioned windows and finials add a touch of elegance.

Centre, left: Large symmetrical farmhouse, built in 1675, with farm buildings attached, at Earl Sterndale in the Derbyshire Peak District.

Centre, right: Solid brick farmhouse with timber-framing, suggesting 17th-century origins, at Stert, Wiltshire.

Above left: Fashionable, stone-built Georgian farmhouse at Chelmorton, Derbyshire.

Above right: Farmhouse dated 1804, Ippollitts, Hertfordshire. An example of the elegant face that the early 19th-century farmer wanted to present to the world – putting him on a social par with the vicar or doctor.

Typical example of a refronted farm Willingale, Essex, the work probably being carried out in the late 18th or early 19th century. The side elevation, below, shows the older, less symmetrical structure which probably dates from the 17th century or possibly even earlier.

emphasis was on symmetry. The farmhouse had become two rooms deep. The outshut, with its continuous catslide roof, was enlarged to make a proper second storey. This produced the 'double-pile' plan, two storeys high front *and* back. Sometimes the two-room depth was marked by a double-pitched roof with a valley between. The half-storey attic, generally used for labourers' and house servants' sleeping quarters, was sometimes pushed up to a full further storey.

Accommodation for servants was more often to be found in a separate service wing. Often they did not have the benefit of a window, since the window tax levied in 1696, and not lifted until 1851, exempted only the apertures of dairies or cheese rooms (provided they were marked as such) and not those used for domestic purposes.

As the farmer moved apart from those he employed, and up the social scale, his wife's tasks and her own view of their standing was changing (an important factor in the design of a house which was, after all, largely her province). Back in the mid-sixteenth century, Fitzherbert had listed the duties of a farmer's wife: as well as baking and brewing, she was expected to help winnow the corn, drive and fill dung carts and to help out at the corn mill. Presumably this was a small family farm but on many medium-sized holdings she was also in charge of the dairy, the pigsties (which went with the former, since skimmed milk was the pigs' prerogative) and poultry. There was a custom that anything earned from the poultry was a perk for the farmer's wife herself. Her role was far from insignificant; as Caird said,

> We think we are not wrong in saying that the farmer's wife in Cheshire is the most important person in the establishment; the cheese, which is either made by her, or under her directions, forming the produce of two-thirds or three-fourths of the farm; the remaining fraction of which comprises the business of the farmer.

Still, not all farmers' wives were content to remain with their elbows in the whey. Parson Woodforde drily observed the pretensions of a local rising star. In 1797 he wrote, 'Mrs. Howlett was at Church and exhibited for the first time, a black Vail over her Face. Times must be good for Farmers when their Wives can dress in such Stile.' John Clare's poem about the farmer's daughter described the same kind of pretensions.

The house was keeping pace with such aspirations. Many a solid seventeenth-century farmhouse was given a new eighteenth-century front of brick or, better still, of stone, to confer architectural dignity and an indication that fashions were not unobserved in the provinces. Sometimes the new elevation is an effective disguise but the room plans and particularly the asymmetrical placing of chimney stacks are good indications of what has occurred. As Eric Mercer puts it, the house was developing in 'stages on the road to a fashionable residence'. In the richer areas, by the late eighteenth century, there was relative uniformity in the three bay, two-and-a-half or three-storey, double-pile farmhouse type. Gables had gone; a more or less classical façade was *de rigueur* and symmetry had been achieved. Many of these new houses were part of the landscape of Parliamentary enclosure – new farmsteads out in the fields, far from the village. Although Beatson knew of 'many respectable and worthy farmers, whose manner and conversation entitle them to the best accommodation', not everyone was to find the Parliamentary enclosures to their advantage. Many observers chronicled the difficulties of country people. The Rev. William Cole, writing in 1766 from his Buckinghamshire parish, described the problems of Will Wood, who had left home because of his worries at finding a house and farm once he was married to 'Henry Travel's daughter, the prettiest girl in the parish'. Cole comments, 'The times are so hard, small farms so difficult to be met with, the Spirit of Enclosing and accumulating Farms together, making it very difficult for young People to marry as was used.' Elsewhere in the parish 'several farmers' sons are forced to live at Home with their fathers, though much wanting to marry and settle, for want of proper Places to settle at.' He lamented 'the baleful Practice of Inclosures'. However, by the end of the eighteenth century the more fortunate farmer in the richer farming areas was likely to be living in an architect-designed farmhouse, a tenant on one of the great improved estates.

Anticipating the needs of this new section of society, Daniel Garrett's book of farmhouse patterns, published in 1747, ran into three editions over a thirty-year period. In various sizes, his farms were always compact and answered Arthur Young's requirement for 'sufficiency of room for lodging conveniently a large family and as many servants as the farm requires'. Another author, Beatson, thought that general characteristics should be uniformity (ornament was unnecessary), large windows and a site well away from the farm buildings – thus avoiding the hazard of fire and the 'disagreeableness of living in a dunghill'. Making what might seem a statement of the obvious he felt that 'a neat small commodious dwelling-house is fully more comfortable than a large dismal one . . .'; he had in mind 'those gloomy preposterous ruinous buildings now a disgrace to almost every part of the kingdom'.

Set in 1799, George Eliot's *Adam Bede* described just such a 'ruin'. Hall Farm was a romantic vision of red brick, softened by dusty, pale lichens. An ancient manor house, it had become the farmhouse; the former parlour, now too big for the needs of the farmer or his wife, housed the sacks of corn and bales of wool. Activity centred principally on the kitchen and the farmyard.

Many of these derelict houses were quite probably the fine expression of sixteenth- and seventeenth-century skills and confidence; perhaps badly maintained, certainly out of fashion, they proved that the turn-of-the-century building boom 100 years before had left behind it a considerable legacy. There had been little need to add to the stock of farmhouses until the Agricultural Revolution began to require new buildings to match its new agriculture. As mentioned above, refronting the house was often sufficient gesture to the winds of change. Yeoman farmers and country squires were not progressives. Squire Hamley, in Mrs. Gaskell's *Wives and Daughters*, was one such. He 'By continuing the primitive manners and customs of his forefathers, the squires of the eighteenth century, did live more as a yeoman, when such a class existed'. His estate was only 800 acres or so – 'there was many a greater landowner in the country' – but 'they had not increased their estate for centuries; they had held their own, if even with an effort, and had not sold a rood of it for the last hundred years or so. But they were not an adventurous race. They never traded, or speculated, or tried agricultural improvements . . .'

The architect-designed farmhouse

Farm on the Grafton estate, Northamptonshire: one of a number all built in a similar style in the early 1840s. The house resolutely turns its back on the buildings behind. Such farmhouses and their well planned buildings were often rewards for good tenants.

Nevertheless, the planned farmstead, and the architect-designed farmhouse that was part of it, represented the modern spirit abroad. These were the farms commissioned by the landowner, possibly designed by the agent, and tenanted by the kind of man already described by Beatson.

The fashions that were followed were those pulsing through the world of architecture and they pandered to the fancies of the owner of the estate. Soon the vocabulary introduced by the important architects of the period, the

brothers Adam, Sir John Soane and many others, filtered into the repertoire of the builders. (They could always refresh their memories at the pattern book fountain. In her thesis, Eileen Spiegel mentions that at least forty-five books containing designs for farmhouses or labourers' cottages were printed between 1727 and 1810 alone.)

A little later, the early Victorian builders and surveyors between them (with a little help from the engineers and architects) were in charge of designing the farmstead, and the house that accompanied the excesses of 'high farming' was generally a mild enough tribute to the Gothic or Tudor styles. Gables had crept back and the farm cottages often resembled the smaller eighteenth-century, double-pile farmhouse pivoted half round, so that the roof-valley ran between the two halves, rather than along the divide behind. Standardization of house type, reached almost a century earlier in the mansions of the great landowners and still far off for the cottage, heralded the farmer as an equal in many respects with his professional colleagues in the village – the clergyman or doctor. Though there were distinct social and economic differences between farmers, in the lowland areas of the country few fell below a certain standard. Things were, however, very different elsewhere.

Hippolyte Taine spotted the gradations in living style that were by then characteristic. A farmer with 100 acres kept a spotless house, he observed. 'I have seen nothing better in the regions of Utrecht or Amsterdam. The farmer's wife told me that every year the inside walls are whitewashed, that the stone flags of the floor are scrubbed once a week.' The farmer with 300 acres had a fine house with a sixteenth-century staircase and antique pieces. The farmer with 600 acres had a drawing room furnished in the Parisian style and a conservatory.

The farmer's wife in her veil, or those families so frequently mocked by other observers for their pretensions in taking the waters or sending their children to grand schools, represented the upper extreme of the farmer's social aims. The great landowner and the gentleman farmer, dabbling in rather than pursuing agriculture, were largely outside the picture. To begin with, they did not live in farmhouses. At the opposite pole was the wife of the small dairy farmer in the Yorkshire Dales or on the fringes of the industrial centres. Her role had changed little since Fitzherbert's description of her work, and her housing was a simple reflection of her daily life working on the farm and the basic needs of her family.

The traditional farmhouse

Despite the changes and improvements being carried out in the richer farming areas in the seventeenth and eighteenth centuries, little had changed in the traditional small farmsteads of upland areas or those of predominantly pastoral lowland farming areas. Farming and domestic life were most closely linked on such farmsteads, and kitchen and laundry, pantry and servants' rooms (if there were such) were linked to the essential rooms of farming activity.

Prime among these was the dairy, usually attached to the north side of the house and slightly sunk to ensure coolness. Sometimes there was a window connecting it to the kitchen for ease of supervision. Louvred windows allowed ventilation and surfaces would all be stone or slate. Plastered walls, lime-washed like the granary to avoid dust building up, gave the room a clinical cleanliness. In Gloucestershire, Marshall commented, the floors were scrubbed with fresh herbs every two weeks – much as lavender was swept over town-house floors at the same period. Elsewhere in the house would be a cheese chamber: there the cheeses remained until they were marketable, being turned twice weekly. In large establishments, a water-powered device carried out the job. This cheese room was often on the first floor, sometimes over the kitchen. Some larger establishments had a number of rooms devoted to dairying, each with a separate function. Robert Adam's design for a farmhouse at Kedleston in Derbyshire included three cheese rooms in the attics.[3] Eventually the combined pressures of mechanization, legislation and standardization drove the dairy first out of the house, and then out of the farm.

In remote areas, other rooms within the house had specialized uses, including the space for keeping meat over winter months; the cellar in which, on smaller farms, the root crop was usually kept; and, more recently, some kind of office or pay desk for the paperwork of farming. The more remote the farm, the greater the need for storage, for there might be long periods in which the valley or dale was inaccessible to the outer world.

Labourers' cottages and conditions
While the house of the small farmer remained little changed, and his labour force probably shared his roof, the tendency on estates where the tenants had been provided with new houses was for tied cottages to be built for the labourers. The cottages implied a combination of motives; as Nathaniel Kent pointed out to Coke of Norfolk in 1789, 'I owe I think it as necessary to provide plain and comfortable habitations for the Poor as it is to provide comfortable and convenient buildings for cattle.' It was, he pointed out, to the landlord's advantage to have a labour force 'permanently fixed to the soil'; they were unlikely to risk their good fortune by 'joining in occasional tumults but will on the contrary be the best props a farmer can lean upon in case of any such calamity and will be the least likely to become a burden upon the parish.'[4] This was not a new idea; Robert Walpole had provided double cottages, farmhouses and almshouses at New Houghton in Norfolk sixty years before.

To a conscientious landlord, the cottages and the new farmhouses were as essential as the newly drained fields, the experimental crops and the carefully bred livestock. At Holkham, according to Arthur Young, the scene expressed 'the diffusion of happiness, an overflow of wealth that gilds the whole country and tells the traveller, in a language too expressive to be misunderstood, *we approach the residence of a man, who feels for others as well as for himself.'*[5] The buildings may have been the second stage in the cycle of agricultural improvements, but without the best farming what use the best buildings? However, Coke and those responsible landlords whose names recur throughout the late eighteenth- and nineteenth-century accounts were the exceptions.

In 1800 the Board of Agriculture began to offer prizes for 'model cottages' and, from its earliest years, the *Journal of the Royal Agricultural Society* paid considerable attention to the subject. The revelations contained in Edwin Chadwick's *Report on the Sanitary Condition of the Labouring Population* (1842), showing that agricultural labourers and their families had an average life expectancy of thirty-three years, compared to that of forty-eight years for their employers, might have been expected to change attitudes.[6] However, it seems that the message did not reach a very wide audience. The conscientious landowners, as before, continued to build houses and cottages to the highest contemporary standards; elsewhere, even during the period of enormous prosperity in agriculture, from the repeal of the Corn Laws in 1846 to the depression of the late 1870s, the farm worker saw little of this golden good fortune.[7] The mean 'bothies', the one-room cabins built by most nineteenth-century Northumberland landowners for their employees, were by no means a unique regional aberration. The most vulnerable sector of all were the 'day labourers', with no security of either work or housing. The 'farm servants', such as bailiffs, ploughmen and those concerned with the livestock, had a better chance since they had tied accommodation, the standard of which depended on the farmer's or landowner's sense of responsibility to his employees.

Housing conditions accurately reflected the attitudes which prevailed; neither the Agricultural Revolution, nor its successor, the Victorian 'high farming' era, were to benefit the farm labourer.

At the end of the eighteenth century wages were still miserable. The Speenhamland system was drawn up to assist the labourers with the price of bread.[8] The scheme came, however, to be an abuse at their expense, as well as at the expense of the small independent farmer who subsidized the wages of labourers for his rich neighbour, the local large landowner, with his contributions to the poor rate. Its outcome was the constant nineteenth-century menace of the workhouse.

By the nineteenth century there were in most parts of the country two distinct groups concerned with agriculture within the village. One group consisted of the landowners, usually shadowy figures rarely seen, of whom 7,000 owned four-fifths of the country in 1873, the tenant farmers (by 1830, 88 per cent of farmers were tenants although forms of tenure varied widely), and the agents who went between the landowners and tenant farmers. The labourers, from the top level of bailiff or steward down, via shepherd, cattleman and ploughman to the annually hired farm workers, formed the other.

In Flora Thompson's *Lark Rise* we see, over the cottage fence, the labourers scything around the mechanical reaper (a novelty in the 1880s) while the bailiff rode about the fields supervising the itinerant Irish workers who slept in the barn during harvest. The scene characterized the gulf between mechanization and hard physical labour and between the social classes.

In his diary the Rev. Francis Kilvert reported the comments of a lady who, visiting an agricultural meeting in Chippenham in Wiltshire in 1872, was appalled by the 'patronising manner in which labourers were preached at', old people kept standing while 'their betters' sat on well-cushioned chairs.

The picture today

Since the nineteenth-century agricultural depression, very few new cottages have been added to the stock of village housing (for those employed in farming, that is) and the farmer living in a house less than a century old is rare indeed. His house may be much changed but the chances are that its foundations range between old and ancient.

Where new houses *have* been built, the anomalies of planning often direct that the old house be unoccupied and, therefore, demolished or decayed beyond retrieval. Not much architectural talent has been displayed in the art of designing farmhouses in the twentieth century – ironically cottages are often better planned.

The farmhouse, as it is used today, has little connection with the farm itself. It might contain the office but nothing more of agricultural significance. Apart from convenience, there is nothing that ties the farmer to the farmstead; indeed many have already left. In some cases the farmhouse is in other hands, in some it has already disappeared. Farm cottages have also gone the same way, now that the agricultural workforce is so small, and dropping further every year. Often they represent wasted housing since they are too expensive to repair in return for controlled rents, and before long they crumble away.

Ancient farmhouses have a quality which comes from more than mere beauty of materials, site or architecture. It is perhaps the quality of continuity which imbues them that provides the explanation – the idea that until recently generation upon generation of farmers' wives had made butter in the dairy or salted meat in the kitchen, and that the conversation has centred almost immemorially on the same subjects – on the weather, the size of the wheat ears and foot rot.

The Rev. Francis Kilvert lovingly described the cottages and farmhouses in his part of Radnorshire. One such house in particular seems to encapsulate the marriage between the place and its function:

> At last I found my way up a rich green orchard and through a gate into the fold sheltered by some noble sycamores. The farmhouse, long, low and yellow-washed, looked towards the N.E. The house is said to be the oldest inhabited building in these parts. It stands high above the Arrow on its green mount, embosomed and almost hidden by its sycamores and other trees. In a dark secluded recess of the wood near the river bank an ice-cold never-failing spring boils up out of the rock . . . In the hot summer days Louie and the other girls take the butter down the steep bank, across the Arrow and make up the butter in the wood by the icy spring. Then they bring the butter up and it remains as if it had been iced.

The Farm Buildings

From Tradition to Innovation

'Not to build anything but what will be really useful', the advice given by an eighteenth-century pattern book author, has, in fact, always been the aim of the farmer. People who dabbled in farming might build follies and eye-catchers; the real farmer, whether landowner, tenant or freeholder, built what he needed and what suited his purpose. Function has always governed the form of traditional farm buildings.

Designed above all to shelter and protect, they have a rationale and an implicit link with the farming process. For this reason the farmstead, along with the cottage, is the epitome of vernacular building – built from materials to hand, in the way that best suited needs. Ingenuity and practicality were all that was required.

In this section, the buildings are grouped by function, as the various crops and types of livestock each dictated relatively specialized structures. Because of the interconnecting links in the farming chain, some functions could be best combined in the same building or, at least, in linked structures. The farmhouse was part of the chain – but very much a separate entity.

The commonplace buildings of the medieval farm go practically unrecorded. Chaucer mentions barns, cowsheds, dairies. We know they existed; we must guess at what they looked like and how they were built. It is reasonable to assume that they shared with cottages of the period the same structural characteristics as a bird's nest: branches, straw and earth were the raw materials. No doubt in some cases more advanced methods and materials were used; but they have not survived either.

Inventories, an early rich source for social historians, are patchy on the subject.[1] Sometimes the farm implements and stock are listed minutely without mention of the buildings in which they were housed. Gervase Markham was an exception among the important writers on husbandry when, around the turn of the seventeenth century, he described in detail the design and requisites of a cart-shed. He gave his advice based on 'English practices, both certaine, easie and cheape: differing from all former and forraine experiments, which eyther agreed not with our Clime, or were too hard to come by, or over-costly, to little purpose . . .' The interest in this preamble is the reference to foreign ideas. Northern Europe was thought to be advanced in matters of husbandry and the theories of France or Flanders were eagerly followed. At the time of the Civil War in the 1640s, many landowners forced abroad used their time to good effect to learn about foreign methods.

The stirrings of the Agricultural Revolution

As the population increased, and foreign and home demand grew, the exhortations of the writers began to bear fruit. Even the most conservative of yeoman farmers could not remain entirely untouched by the stream of advice being published, nor by the pressures and appeal of the rapidly increasing market.

By the latter years of the seventeenth century, at the beginning of the revolution in agriculture, the literature was becoming a massive flood; and the setting up of the Royal Society was an important step towards the establishment of these new ideas. Ubiquitous figures such as John Evelyn[2] turned their minds to husbandry – he wrote notable works on both soil and cider – and this stream of knowledge was, as Trevelyan succinctly puts it, 'a constant stimulant but often a sore puzzle to the practical farmer'. Productivity was improving meantime, and the grain surplus achieved in the latter decades of the seventeenth century was encouraged by the Corn Bounties.[3]

Meanwhile, the livestock population – cattle, oxen and horses – was growing. New root crops and higher grain yields allowed them to live through the winter. It was an ascending spiral and required more land and better methods, were it to continue. From the end of the sixteenth century onwards, improved buildings began to play their part; they might be traditional in structure but they were better built from stronger materials, to sustain a more business like kind of farming. It was from these vernacular buildings that the more carefully designed structures (detailed in the second part of this chapter) evolved.

Medieval tithe barn, Frocester Court, built for the Abbot of Gloucester around 1300. Constructed of local limestone, it is 186ft long, 30ft wide and has 13 bays. There are several other fine barns in the Severn Valley – notably at Ashleworth and Hartpury.

Barns
The importance of the buildings was conferred by their usefulness and the barn has always been pre-eminent – even where grain is not the principal concern.

The barn encompasses a vast range of building types. At the upper end was the immense tithe barn or monastic grange: factory and warehouse in one, it has little to do with the farmstead. It was used to house the tithes (tithe means one tenth), which were levied to support Church, clergy and, in principle, the poor. Tithes were already in existence at the Norman Conquest, having become a legal obligation in the tenth century. Since they were taken in kind, the tithe barns that were built to house them had to be enormous. (Not every large barn described today as a tithe barn was in fact built as such. The term has become loosely applied and much misused.)

In architectural terms, the tithe barn is merely the most showy (and ancient) of existing barns. As a symbol of manorial or ecclesiastical privilege, it epitomized the commercial aspirations of the landowners, as the cathedrals mirrored the spiritual aspirations of *their* builders. The tithe barn echoed the style of the monastery and borrowed the proportions of the church. It multiplied the dimensions of the humble farm barn: where the latter had three or five bays, the tithe barn had eight or ten; where the ordinary corn barn had a single threshing floor, the tithe barn had two or three. It was constructed from the best materials to hand, built by master carpenters and masons. Medieval parish church and tithe barn still stand; medieval cottage and farm buildings have long ago crumbled back into the ground.

Yet corn barns incorporated the principles of the tithe barn on a reduced scale – to harbour the corn crop and provide shelter for the separation of grain from straw. The basic requirements were a sturdy shell, with a considerable roof height, generous width, adequate ventilation and large doors to admit the load, whether carried by a pitchfork, a horse with panniers or a waggon.

The particular features of the hay barn in upland areas were induced by differing needs: the wetter climate, demanding more protection from porches, deep eaves or sills; the often uneven terrain (to be taken advantage of for its useful change of level, as in the bank barn); more crucially, the need for storage space for hay and implements sometimes turned the structure into a multi-purpose building.

So, too, in lowland areas of relatively small-scale farming, where the farmer often had other part-time employment, the barn would be used for storage of all kinds of things as well as housing livestock and perhaps farm servants. These variations will be dealt with in more detail in the regional sections, but it is important to consider the barn as a flexible element of the farmstead, turned by the farmer to whatever use seemed appropriate. Only in the arable areas of the country were its functions neatly confined to those of storage and processing of corn. In pastoral areas barns were designed for the hay crop with perhaps just enough space for the corn and straw required for domestic and livestock needs.

The size of the barn was determined by farm acreage and yield. Thus few barns have remained unaltered over the centuries. Certain periods have been advantageous for growing cereals; for example, at the time of the Corn Bounties or when, in the early eighteenth century, dramatically increased yields had been brought about by improved farming methods, especially in fertilization and seed corn quality. Conversely, barns have fallen into disuse in times of recession – such as the disastrous aftermath of Free Trade in the late Victorian period, which had such savage impact on the efficient corn-growing counties of eastern England. [4] At such a time a barn might have been adapted for other uses – or abandoned – but not structurally altered. A study of the barns at Manor Farm, Cogges, in Oxfordshire, shows the various alterations that took place as farming decreed flexibility in successive generations. [5]

Decisions had to be made by the farmer which determined the dimensions and form of the building. How high would waggon loads be, how many would approach at one time, how big need the threshing floors be, and how many?

The only constant factors were the two separate areas, one in which to store unthreshed sheaves, the other threshed corn; a good hard surface for the threshing floor; and the two opposing doors, designed to give maximum draught utilizing the prevailing wind as far as possible (with a knee-high board placed across the open entrance to keep out stray farm animals and fowls). Stone flagging or sound timber was preferred; beaten earth or even brick or tiles allowed the possibility of an unsavoury dusty additive to the grain. Writing in the late eighteenth century, Arthur Young thought clay floors most unsatisfactory as 'a bright sample of corn cannot be had from off them.' He favoured wood: oak planks, two or three inches thick, were ideal. However, by the end of the century oak was getting expensive – a few years later Marshall suggested 'weedling plants' for the purpose, anything else being a waste of good wood.

The winter work with flails, beating the corn inside the barn for hour upon hour, was an arduous business – one of the rituals of the rural labourer's life. Yet the low cost of labour meant that even after widespread mechanization in the mid-nineteenth century, following the introduction of the threshing machine, the traditional methods endured. It often cost less to maintain a band of men than horses; as late as 1874 the Rev. Francis Kilvert, heard 'the old familiar sound once so common, the sound of the flail on the barn floor. I had not heard it for years. I looked in at the barn door and found a man threshing out his barley.'

However, in terms of change in the structure of the barn, the threshing machine (to which we return later) required only small modifications. In fact, many of the improvements suggested by Arthur Young, novel as they were, required only adaptation of existing buildings, or some additional building. One such was an idea for the addition of a chaff house, separated from the barn by sliding windows through which the threshers pushed the corn.

The practice of using different barns for different crops was not, however, a novel one. For instance, the two thirteenth-century barns at Cressing, Essex, were known as the Wheat and Barley barns. Wheat was the principal crop in the prosperous arable regions of the South and thus was vouchsafed the finest barn on most farms. Barley (destined largely for the maltings or farm brewhouse) was kept in a smaller structure.

In the wetter, upland areas where corn was grown of necessity for home consumption, the grain had to be dried and a kind of kiln was developed, much like that used for hops, with warmth and ventilation. Once the upland areas began to obtain grain from elsewhere, importing it from arable areas better suited to the cultivation of corn crops, these kilns disappeared. In the mid-eighteenth century, an internal room was incopropated into the barn in some areas. [6] Built of brick and plastered, it was used to keep threshed corn before winnowing. This 'corn hole', as it was known, introduced a further distinction into the use of space inside the barn, an adaptation for functional reasons.

Straw was a central commodity of any farm with even an acre or two of grain. It not only fed the livestock but provided their bedding, and was trodden in for precious manure, as well as being used for roofing. Of course, its utilization varied from farm to farm, but apart from grain, straw was the key to the

Three-tier barn at Ashtead, Surrey, probably dating from the late 18th century. The top tier was used for hay and general stores, the middle one for winter feed and the ground level for housing cattle and other animals.

This combination of hay store and cow-house was a useful answer to the problem of storing winter fodder and feeding cattle in the cold and wet months but is a rare building type for the southern counties. It is generally found in the bank barns of the Lake District and the field barns of the Yorkshire Dales.

Above: A field barn, Yorkshire. Ranging from the tiny upland barn of the Pennines to the grandiose architect-designed versions on progressive estates such as Holkham (see p. 165), field barns provided storage and protection for animals, especially in cold or exceptionally wet weather.

Top right: 19th-century field barn and fold yard at Hinton on the Green, Gloucestershire. As field and farm sizes increased with improvements, in terms of power, crops and quality of livestock and size of herds, the need for outlying sets of buildings became greater.

Right: Weather-boarded hay barn near Wisborough Green, West Sussex.

elaborate cycle of pre-industrial farming. It was generally kept under cover once it came off the fields. The rickyard was a later development – a response first to higher productivity and the increased volume of straw to be stored between harvests, and second to mobile threshing machines.

Although a large corn barn was primarily agricultural in function, it was usually the grandest secular building in the village, apart from the manor house, and it therefore played an important social role. It made a perfect village hall. When a Lancashire landowner, Squire Blundell, finished the important job of marling, or fertilizing, his land in 1712 (it happened only at twenty-two-year intervals), he 'began to teach the eight Sword Dancers their Dance which they are to Dance at ye Flowering of my Marl-pit', after which 'they had music and danced it in my Barn.' Four years before the construction of the barn itself had given cause for celebration; after the roof-tree of the building had been put up, there was dancing and drinking to commemorate the 'rearing' of the barn.

An empty barn could serve other purposes apart from village junketings. Kilvert recounted a scene in March 1870 (late enough in the winter for the straw supply to be much depleted) in a barn near Clyro in Herefordshire. He was walking near a farm when he noticed that

> There was a stir about the house and yard. They had killed a fat stall-fed heifer yesterday and a party of people much interested in the matter . . . were busy cutting up the carcass in the barn. A man went to and from the barn to the house with huge joints of beef having first weighed them on the great steelyard which hangs at the barn door.

After that the joints were salted and stored in the farmhouse.

Right: A timber-framed barn with grain bins at Sandon, Hertfordshire.

Far right: Timber-framed barn at Great Thurlow, Suffolk. A large threshing barn, it is probably of 18th-century construction. The entrance, with its modern 'up and over' door, would have given on to the threshing floor in the central bay. Originally, matching double doors would have provided the necessary draught. Redundant for its original purpose, the barn now serves as a useful storage place for baled straw, the doors wide enough to admit a trailer.

Above: The brick granary at Tytherington, Wiltshire, *c*. 1810, is raised on plinths to protect the grain from vermin and other predators. The segmental gable provides space for pigeons to roost while adding a touch of elegance.

Right: The granary at Peper Harow, Surrey, built around 1600. It is a particularly fine example of the purpose-built granary-cum-cart-shed of early date. Tile-hung in the tradition of the region, it has glazed windows and louvred ventilation points. The space for carts has proved suitable for modern equipment. The granary rests on 25 timber supports and is completely square.

Granaries

The grain itself was too precious to leave in the barn. It had to be secure from light fingers and rodent hunger. The purpose-built granary, as we know it, is principally a late seventeenth-century development, although examples do exist from the Tudor period and many must have disappeared without a trace. On most farms, however, the crop was housed in wooden chests in the farmhouse – probably in the attic. John Worlidge, in his *Systema Agriculturae*, published in 1681, wrote 'Binns or Hutches for corn may be placed on Pins . . . but great caution must be used that no stick ladder or other thing lean against these places, lest the Mice find the way to come where you would not have them.' The soundly built eighteenth-century granary always stood raised from the ground, supported either on wooden legs or, more effectively, on staddle stones or a low brick plinth. Worlidge's 'Vermine and Children of Darkness' would be deterred from even the most ingenious ascent. The same author also proposed an elaborate arrangement whereby a granary might be built with more than one storey, the grain being pushed downwards through a chute in the floor.

The granary was used only for part of the year, after harvest and before sale. It was useful to have extra capacity in case the market was down, in which case the farmer could wait a bit longer for prices to rise. In 1799, Parson Woodforde of Norfolk – like most country parsons he was something of a part-time farmer, cultivating his glebe lands and marketing the produce – could hardly give his barley away. 'The Corn Merchants said that it was at present such a glut that they had almost as soon not have it as have it.' Such were the vicissitudes that in 1801 he was reporting 'an enormous Price' for his wheat; yet when the farmer benefited, the people without land suffered. Woodforde went so far as to 'sincerely wish it might be cheaper e'er long for the benefit of the Poor who are distressed on that Account . . . Pray God! send us better Times and all People better.'

If a granary was large enough, other dry crops, such as hops, could be stored there as well. Grain for sale had to be distinguished from that for seed corn and home consumption. Seed corn, usually the heaviest grain, was conserved with special care. One manual suggested deal boards to separate different grains and poured scorn on the farmer who, possessed of a perfectly good granary, lost his crop through badly made sacks – 'a disgraceful bit of negligence, the sole consequence of the "want of a stitch in time"', the author smugly cracked.

The relatively small storage capacity needed meant that the granary could be incorporated into another building. If it was not a single-storey structure (of brick, stone, tile-hung, timber-framed or weather-boarded, depending on its location), it could form the upper storey of, usually, the cart-shed. Livestock sheds were found unsuitable since the noxious gases from below would affect the grain. In this arrangement the granary was approached by a flight of external steps and had an upper loading door. Another version, taken to elaborate lengths in Herefordshire, consisted of a purpose-built wing of the farmhouse that retained the features of a domestic building.[7] Wherever the granary might be, strong doors and well-fastened windows (later glazed or

barred for additional protection) were most important. Parson Woodforde, like many, was robbed by petty thieves. Yet despite the valuable contents of stable and corn room, he was surprised that they contented themselves with a hatchet, hook bridle and hedging gloves. They were caught and imprisoned for three years.

Against the smaller, greedier four-legged intruders, cat and owl holes were often provided. In fact farming manuals devote considerable space to the question of providing access points for cats into both barns and granaries to deal with marauding rats and mice. One suggestion was a special entrance to the space beneath the timber boards (nasty surprise for the thief). Equally,

damp caused considerable waste. Ackermann's *Repository*, published in 1809, during the Napoleonic Wars, included letters from 'an Economist' on the loss of produce brought about by badly made floors. Raised floors with ventilation holes could 'save a million in corn every year'; vermin could be dealt with by 'giving grimalkin, their mortal enemy, an opportunity to surround them'. Plastered walls and ceilings reduced dust, keeping the stored produce purer.

Cart-sheds

As the buildings used for crop storage evolved, there was also a growing need to protect the increasingly sophisticated and valuable array of farm implements from the ravages of the weather and the interference of farm animals. Implements made partly of metal were being introduced, and so rust was an added problem. Either as a separate building or as a natural accompaniment to the granary, the cart-shed thus became more and more ubiquitous.

Although some agricultural writers thought a lean-to against the back wall of the barn perfectly adequate, Burke suggested that cart-sheds should open away from the farmyard so that cattle could not get in 'and do mischief'. Writing earlier, at the turn of the seventeenth century, Gervase Markham had given a sensible description of a cart-shed:

> The sun does more harm to a Cart than either Wind or Rain. However they are all three Enemies, and are easily prevented by a Cart-shed – which need not cost much; for one may be made with eight Crochets, and as many Spars. It may be covered with Bavin wood, Brakes, Furzes or other Firing . . . under there a Cart is immediately out of Wind and Weather.

Also, he points out, safe from the farmyard hogs.

The carts, waggons and wooden implements of Markham's time were superseded by the larger and more valuable pieces of machinery of later centuries and so the cart-house grew in importance.

Housing for livestock

Proper housing for cattle was an early concern from the large medieval monastic 'vaccaries' onwards. Oxen, whether they were used as draught animals or were being fattened for slaughter, required their own accommodation too. Thomas Tusser, Suffolk farmer and sixteenth-century writer on agriculture, stated the position clearly:

> The housing of cattle, while winter doth hold,
> Is good for all such as are feeble and old.
> It saveth much compas, and many a sleep,
> And spareth the pasture for walk of thy sheep.[8]

The cow-house that Arthur Young prescribed was to be roomy with 'yoaks, ties, hooks and bings' (the latter were loose-box compartments for holding calves, a maximum of five in principle). Adjoining it, or overhead, should be spaces for both hay and straw. The bull always had his own regal pen.

Above left: A neatly thatched straw rick and waggon-shed at Lacock, Wiltshire – the home of William Fox Talbot, who took this photograph in the 1840s.

Left: Kent farm, oil painting by Robert Hills, *c.* 1813. A lean-to shelter for cattle, typical of this period. It protects the animals and provides a handy store for the bundles of pea-sticks, straw or bracken that form the roofing. As needed they could be tossed down for the livestock.

The ox, with his wide horns, required a stall large enough to turn in. The yoke determined the width (it was also the measuring device of the bays in a barn, each bay being two pairs of oxen wide). Although the ox was slowly superseded by the horse in the progressive arable farming areas during the Agricultural Revolution, it lingered on in remoter areas of mixed farming. It was slower but much hardier than the horse and required less fodder over winter, a crucial consideration. Kilvert saw some in the mid-1870s near Kington St. Michael, in Herefordshire. 'I fell in with a team of red oxen, harnessed, coming home from plough with chains rattling and the old plough-man riding the fore ox.'

That cattle need a warm and dry feeding place was early established. Every farmer knew that cold beasts ate more and fattened less well. However, the need for light and ventilation was not recognized until much more recently. The traditional cow-byre, with its regional variations in the tying and placing of animals, was a dank place, with gullies for manure collection and a passage for access to the feeding racks. Where there was a loft overhead, the hay was pushed down through a trap-door directly into the racks. The farmer or cow-man scrambled upstairs on a flimsy ladder inside the shed. The animals were separated by partitions and although wood was used widely, stone, slate, brick and, later, iron were more practical – wearing better against the rubbing of the animals' heads and flanks and against their tendency to chew anything they could bury their teeth in. Rubbing posts were often provided, and failing these, at least rounded doorways or pillars.

The condition of cattle and oxen was very much dependent upon their well-being – both physical and mental. Thus adequate housing was crucial and it was not until a more scientific approach to farming was adopted in the eighteenth century that the consequences of earlier mistakes could be seen.

In winter, milking took place in the cattle sheds. In summer months it could easily be done in the fields. Kilvert recorded the picturesque scene of a boat loaded with churns returning from some distant pasture. It was primarily for convenience that milking was done indoors; if the cow-house was close to the dairy, it made life easier for the farmer's wife and dairymaid.

There were other reasons why the cow- or ox-house should be close to the farmhouse. If roots were stored in the latter, then it was convenient that the two should be adjacent; calves which might depend on additional feeding also needed foodstuffs prepared in the house. Later on, the cattle housing moved close to the root house – for the same reasons.

As we have seen, where farms were small and the husbandry was mixed, a dual-purpose building made sense. Small amounts of grain, hay and food-stuffs could easily be housed within the same space as a number of cattle and a pony. The aisled barn frequently had cattle stalls along the edges, sometimes for considerable numbers. In addition, in the southern examples, the milder climate meant that covered livestock accommodation was generally required only in emergencies, for sick animals or for those newly born.

The housing of cattle was constantly under discussion. Some favoured a loose foldyard with food provided in racks on the outer walls and lean-to shelter around the perimeter. Others thought both a compartmentalized cow-

Above: Arthur Young's suggestion for a byre or 'ox-shade', as he called it, from *The Farmer's Guide*, Vol. II, 1770.

Below: A cattle byre in the Meifod Valley, Powys, showing the type of conditions in which cattle lived prior to the Agricultural Revolution. In those days, the low ceiling height, single source of light and single passage, doubling as a collection point for milk and manure, were standard.

Right: Traditional Devon linhay (or linney) near Salcombe, Devon. The open-fronted hay store faces south to benefit from all available warmth. Cob has been used at the upper level, pierced to provide nesting places for pigeons. Slabs of granite have been used to support the loft.

shed and open provision were necessary; of course the scale of farming largely determined what the farmer chose to build.

The foldyard provided a means for instant manure – as the dung was trodden into the straw. The more straw that was heaped in, the better. Otherwise the manure from the cattle housing would be taken to the midden, a sunken area centrally placed and surrounded by a raised, paved path to make the job of wheeling barrowloads of dung in wet weather slightly less unpleasant.

Beatson considered that for a farm depending on grazing animals very few farm buildings were needed. Walls with a temporary roofing of hay or pea stalks would do nicely; as mentioned before, the farmer could then store the bundles there and toss them down as fodder one by one. Arthur Young thought otherwise. Many farms, he observed, had scattered buildings and no enclosed yard. Cattle should be kept in, since outside they endangered young spring crops and trod pasture grass into quagmires. According to the size of the herd, one or two yards should be provided and it was essential that water be provided – ideally a nearby pond, dug specially if need be and well sealed with a bottom of stone, gravel or chalk.

Young's words were directed at the aspiring progressive farmer; Beatson, writing a few years later, addressed himself to a wider, less affluent readership. These divergencies in view reflected long-held differences in the farming world about the relative virtues of keeping animals under cover or out in the fields – the two arguments are still advanced to this day.

Among the various animals on the farm, both in the past and today, sheep require the least housing and least specialized accommodation. The question of shelter for sheep over the hard winter periods has, however, always been a lively one for farmers. In early medieval times the sheep was primarily a dairy animal but as the emphasis shifted to its wool, it became a hardier, upland creature. A further shift to its use for meat has led to the breeding of different kinds of sheep, requiring other forms of shelter. The only constant has been

A midden on a moorland valley farm at Bransdale in North Yorkshire. It is generously deep to allow manure to be piled up until required for distribution.

the need for shelter during lambing, which has led to many an outlying building to provide warmth for the ewe and for the wretched shepherd.

In exposed upland areas of moor or rocky hillsides, hurdles and makeshift lean-to shelters have usually been sufficient, kept small in order that the animals could huddle together and share their body heat. Sometimes the sheep had accommodation of their own; the 'stell' consisted of a circular wall with a single entrance, a hay rick and racks for the hay. It was positioned downhill in order that the snow, trampled to water, would easily drain off.

On downlands where the sheep would be kept on cornland to fold or manure it – 'moving dunghills' as one writer termed them – there would be a yard with sheltering lean-to sheds on the perimeter and possibly a proper room for the shepherd, complete with fireplace. Where sheep were being fattened, their warmth was essential: a cold beast is a skinny beast.

Transhumance, the practice of taking animals to higher regions during summer months (as they still are in Alpine regions), died out slowly but continued until the nineteenth century in Wales; while this practice continued, the buildings (known as shielings in the North and hafods in Wales) included seasonal accommodation for the labourer or farmer and long-term storage for the hay. The shieling or hafod was to become redundant – the farmstead below took over as the year-round base of the farmer.

As the woods and wastelands contracted, the pig was brought into the farmyard. In the 1770s Lord Anson, one of the largest landowners in Staffordshire, had on his estate at Shugborough a 'very complete hoggery', well-slated and including a cold bath, 'for giving occasional washing to the pigs'. The pigsty, in its outward form not one of the more elaborate structures in even the later model farmsteads, allowed for inventiveness in internal fittings. A farm described in *The Builder* in the 1840s had pigsties with 'an outer trough built up, in which the wash is put to feed them and shutters down an inclined plane inside, into the troughs; this requires no straining in the person feeding them, to lift the bucket over the wall' – labour-saving devices for the farmer's wife or dairymaid, in fact. Pigs, because of their dependence on waste products from the dairy, were traditionally 'woman's work' and were always housed near the dairy. Sometimes an elaborate system of pipes carried the skimmed milk to the sties, sometimes the buckets were carried round. Clearly it was important that they should be as close as possible.

Gervase Markham had been an earlier supporter of shelter for pigs: 'a stye for a boar and hogscote for hog' went with 'a roost for thy hens, and a couch for thy dog' in his list of husbandry furniture. Over the centuries various versions of the pigsty emerged; one of the more idiosyncratic was the Welsh conical type, adapted from an ancient structure of uncertain origins. One explanation for housing a pig was that, with less woodland to explore, he became a nuisance in the farmyard. Tusser pointed out that they often made use of cart-sheds: 'Your Hog (a creature extremely fearful of Wind and Rain, and to whom the heat of the sun is pernicious) finds here Shelter and Shade and Wheel to rub against'; the pig was also, he explained, fond of corn stacks and 'will certainly undermine them if he can'. For this reason he suggests keeping 'pease and tares' on the roof of a shed – safe from both pigs and the damp.

Arthur Young's 'hog conveniences' demanded space for each sow and another separate sty for each animal being fattened. 'In a large or even a middling farm, the hog is an animal of great consequence and proper places for keeping him must on no account be overlooked.' Equipment that Young considered necessary included cisterns for the various foods (butter-milk, whey, malt, grains, etc.), which connected via pipes or guttering to the troughs in the sty. In addition, Young points out, 'swine will not fatten without water.' The highest praise of all from Young was accorded to the pig. 'Nothing about a farm will make such quantities of excellent manure as hogs well-managed.' For this reason they needed separate ricks nearby so that they could make the best possible use of the straw.

Together with the pig, and sometimes even sharing their accommodation, poultry were another concern for the farmer's wife. Remnants of feudal practice lingered on in the poultry yard. Hens and eggs were acceptable rental long after the curious stratification of medieval labourer and freeman became a thing of the past.

There really was little need for purpose-built accommodation, for the foraging fowl could always find shelter in a barn or around the cart-shed. Nevertheless, the theorists, ever busily diversifying the range of buildings around the farmyard, began to incorporate a shelter for them too. On larger establishments 'hen-cotes' were provided with individual nesting boxes and little ramps. Since poultry like warmth, it was suggested that flues on the mechanized farmstead could run through the poultry-houses.

Pigeons, however, were quite another matter. The produce of the dovecote had ceased to be feudal privilege in the early seventeenth century. Nevertheless, most farmers provided perching places and nesting holes on a barn or on the gable of the farmhouse. The manure was valuable and the meat an important supplement, especially in winter. Weighed against that was the predatory behaviour of the pigeons, who raided the fields for their nourishment. Better, however, losses from your own birds than from those of the lord of the manor. The medieval incursions of pigeons, rabbits and deer from the feudal domain were a great cause of friction.

Far right, above: Great Coxwell barn, Oxfordshire, built for the Cistercian Abbey of Beaulieu in Hampshire. One of the finest surviving medieval barns in England, it is of Cotswold stone, and is 152ft long and 44ft wide. It dates from the middle of the 13th century, although the doors on the end walls are 18th-century additions, possibly for larger carts. There is a dovecote over the east door and at one time there was a loft in the upper west porch – accommodation for the monk in charge. (The barn is open to the public.)

Far right: The tithe barn at Upper Heyford, Oxfordshire, was built for William of Wykeham, Bishop of Winchester *c.* 1400. It is built of rubble stone, with stone quoins and buttresses, and remains even now in agricultural use. It is encircled by later buildings including a brick-nogged, timber-framed granary.

Overleaf: Great brick barn at Mulbarton, Norfolk. The Dutch gable ends are a familiar feature in this area.

Right: Arthur Young's plan for the arrangement of an ideal piggery, published in the *Farmer's Guide*, Vol. III, 1770.

The fine manorial dovecote is, of course, a building type of particular beauty, which has often survived because of the quality of its materials and construction. Sometimes, in common with other small varieties of farm building, it was a dual-purpose structure combined with barn or granary. More unusually, the dovecote at Chastleton, in Oxfordshire, doubles as a cattle shelter in the midst of the pasture, far from the house and other outbuildings. A three-storey example in Kent had pigs on the ground floor, hens (taking advantage of a change of level) above, entering from the orchard on the opposite side, and doves tucked in overhead.[9]

Whilst pigeon manure was prized, goose dung was thought to be harmful. Still, geese were useful as watch-dogs as well as being a source of food, and were kept in quantity. Like cattle, they were driven over long distances to be sold at fairs, such as the celebrated Nottingham Goose Fair.

An animal that had its own value in the farmyard was the sheepdog. Its accommodation was often in a neat kennel scooped out under the steps leading to the upper storey of the stable or cow-house; tethered there on a long rope it could act as watch-dog (in the absence of geese) and its tiny dry home was adequate for an animal that took a phenomenal amount of exercise in the course of its duties. Many such dog kennels still exist on upland farms.

Horses, which gradually replaced oxen as draught animals on the farm, did not always fare as well. While the farmer's riding horses were generally soundly housed, 'this faithful, this valuable servant' frequently inhabited a 'miserable tottering hovel'. The horse, and its common companion, the goat, deserved better.

More attention was given to the problem of security than of construction. Tusser talks of 'a stable, well planked, with key and with lock', although he also adds 'a rack and a manger, good litter and hay, Sweet chaff, and some

Top left: Pennine landscape of small walled fields and outlying hay barns, Swaledale, North Yorkshire.

Left: Lakeland farm with house and barn and cow-byre sharing the same roof at Kentmere, Cumbria. Small fields provide grazing and hay crops.

Right: Traditional dog kennel on a moorland sheep farm, Bransdale. There are many such kennels, making use of the odd corner in a farmyard, in this area.

provender, every day'. The stable was attractive to pilferers; in a building contract dated 1473 for a combined stable and shippon for Thomas Peyton, lord of the manor at Wixoe, in Suffolk, the security aspect was emphasized.[10] Each window should have four pillars, in order that a child could not squeeze through. Other practical details attended to in later versions of the stable concentrated on the feeding arrangement: a manger, lined with slate (as well as the lower areas of the walls), is easier to keep clean and, an additional advantage, horses cannot grind it.

Any expansion of the stable block denoted the expansion of arable farming brought about by eighteenth-century improvements. An analysis of the stable building at Manor Farm, Cogges, shows alterations in the mid-century to accommodate more working animals and eventually the raising of the single storey block by the addition of a substantial hay loft, with external access stairs. The stable could be identified by its windows: cowsheds did not merit more than crude openings.

Arthur Young had another point to raise about the design of stables. 'In a very large stable there are so many horsekeepers, that it is little more than a gossiping meeting; the horses are not so much attended to, as the fellows chattering, gaming and idleness.' If stables were dotted about, it was more practical for the spreading of manure, as well as encouraging the farm servants to work harder. This seems to have been one piece of advice from Young that few farmers heeded.

The farmyard

All the buildings of the farmstead revolved around the farmyard. As has been described in the section dealing with siting, the particular juxtapositions rarely occurred by accident; as time went on, their relationships were more and more carefully planned. The mid-Victorian grand plan for an elaborate mixed holding would advocate numerous yards, but most farms in reality – even the large ones – favoured a single central point.

Whether it was the rough space that fell between a motley selection of buildings or the four-square purposeful space of the planned farmstead, the yard had a central function. It was here that the manure was collected and distributed to the fields (unless of course the animals folded the fields direct) and frequently the midden was to one side of the yard. Obviously it made sense if the livestock shelters or foldyard were as close as possible and the midden was generally surrounded by a raised, paved path to make it easier for the farmer to fork manure into it from the adjacent buildings. There was very little difference of opinion on the value of manure, but there were some odd notions about it. Some authorities would have it that the manure of the horse was good for cornland, that of cattle for grassland, since in each case that is what they ate.

The farmyard of the small upland farm also harboured the poultry; hens picking around in the dust and geese patrolling were usual and if the pond was nearby, then ducks added to the scene of activity. The flooring of the yard needed to be hard, preferably flagged, since in winter a morass of mud would soon build up. Not only were flagged or cobbled floors easier to clean, but the removal of manure from all areas was made much easier with a firm base. Stone and, later, cast-iron sills at the entrance to livestock sheds allowed feet to be scraped so that muck was not carried around the well-ordered farm.

Good drainage of the yards has always been important; it is easy to imagine, and in fact still easy to find, the farmyard swilling with mud, manure and, today, oil, which each time it rains become more impassable. Thus gullies and proper guttering, enclosed manure collection and proper surfacing remain essential.

The buildings and areas that housed the livestock and crops of the traditional farmstead had marked regional variations, which were emphasized by their local names: for example, 'linhay', 'shippon' and 'byre' are all versions of cowshed or cow-house. In fact the language of the farm tells much of early settlements and early farmers; Kilvert, visiting William Barnes, 'the Poet of England', near Dorchester, heard him tell that the calls used on Wiltshire and Dorset dairy farms were the same as those used for cows in Scandinavia. Like the words, the regional adaptations of the buildings were gradually influenced by outside considerations, but continued to suit local need. There were also many more specialized structures: early forms of kilns and oast houses, for example. These further components of the farm will be discussed in the appropriate regional sections.

Change and Innovation

From the 1770s, every farmer, with the exception of those in remote and impoverished regions, had to admit change. While he was reading about it, a neighbour was already building up his holding, draining his land and passing on the word. Prosperous times allowed him to consider carrying out some innovations of his own, which in turn would encourage the more conservative of *his* neighbours.

Publications were one means of spreading the word. Shows and demonstrations were another. The famous annual shearings at Holkham in Norfolk (at one of which Coke actually sheared some sheep himself) and meetings of the regional societies, of which the Bath and West, founded in 1777, was the first, were to be institutionalized with the founding of the annual Royal Agricultural Show in 1839.[1] Another effective network was the social one. Many of the major landowners met at these occasions as well as in each other's houses. Some of them were also related to each other – Lord Anson at Shugborough, for example, was Coke's son-in-law.

As in everything, there was no better example than a royal one. 'Ralph Robinson' (George III's pseudonym) was a contributor to the *Annals of Agriculture* and a long account of the King's 'rough Jewel', the royal farm at Windsor, appeared in the *Georgical Essays*. It had been taken on in 1791 and consisted of 4,000 acres – much of it forest. Around the Great Park, in which deer and cattle were retained, two farms were set up, Norfolk Farm and Flemish Farm (their names alluding to the kind of rotation which was practised, both variations on the four-course system). Oxen, unusually, were still preferred to horses and some 200 were kept (with forty fattened off each year); they worked in teams of six and lived in open sheds.

The farms were obviously designed to be in the public eye. Methods of
publicity tended to be disingenuous; Arthur Young met Sir Mordaunt Martin
in the midst of the East Anglian countryside, he tells us, gazing over 'a field of
mangel wurzel. Sir Mordaunt is a great advocate of the culture of this plant.' It
is no accident that the meeting was recorded. Young wanted to convey the
information about the novel crop with a light touch, not as a didactic exercise.

Of course, as Nathaniel Kent put it, 'the intelligent farmer will always know
and gather more from practice and observation than he can acquire from
books and study.' The answer came from a Victorian agriculturalist, Philip
Pusey: 'Books will not teach farming, but if they describe the practices of the
best farmers they will make men think, and show where to learn it.'[2] By
whatever means a farmer learned, a great deal was being achieved.

Whether, in building terms, this change was expressed in the adjustment of
existing buildings to new requirements, or in the large-scale planning of new
farmsteads, obviously depended on the size of the enterprise and how it was
financed. Tenant farmers had widely varying arrangements with their landlords, which affected the repair and erection of buildings as it did the system of
tenure.

By the first decade of the nineteenth century the fruits of a peaceful
revolution could be seen; a vastly increased population was being fed off a not
significantly greater area of cultivated land. There had indeed been an Agricultural Revolution.

To an eighteenth- or nineteenth-century eye, the buildings of the farm
could speak volumes about a farmer. As one writer put it, neat buildings mean
neat agriculture. They also spelt out an alliance between innovative landlord,
clever agent and amenable tenant farmer that was, ideally at least, to govern
much of post-Parliamentary enclosure farming. It was this partnership that
produced the great farming estates, such as those in Norfolk, Bedfordshire

Right: The Royal Dairy, designed by G.A. Dean, and built in 1858 for Prince Albert at the Home Farm, Frogmore, Windsor Great Park. The dairy, like many similar buildings of its period, was more ornamental than practical.

and Staffordshire, where currents of thought, and taste, met. On estates such as these, there was a move towards productive and efficient agriculture, on consolidated holdings amidst newly organized landscape. There was the need for new buildings, supplied for the first time by professional architects who were increasingly eager to turn their attention to the design of humbler buildings than had formerly been their 'province' and who were working with theories that ordained a landscape cunningly made more natural than nature itself, those of the Romantic movement and those expounded by the landscape architects as the Picturesque. [3]

The home farm: a place for experiment

The home farm, within the park of a large estate – often in view of the mansion and, therefore, more readily under the influence of the landlord – was the testing ground for a new approach to agriculture, architecture and landscape combined. From here the landlord could commission an architect to design both the house and the farm buildings, organize the landscape into a combination of the pretty and the practical, and run his agricultural enterprise along the newest lines.

The landlord's approach to building might be merely that of constructing a small eye-catching building – such as William Kent's castellated cow shelter at Rousham, in Oxfordshire, built in 1738 – or there might be an opportunity to construct an entire farmstead. The designs of the Adam brothers at Kedleston in Derbyshire or of Capability Brown at Blenheim in Oxfordshire exemplified the new approach to the design of farm buildings within the needs and climate of the Agricultural Revolution.

Some of the distinguished architects employed understood the needs of farming, others patently did not. Although Sir John Soane drew up plans for an oast house, an elaborate hen-house, various dairies and a wide range of farm buildings for a number of wealthy landowner clients, his elegant cowshed, built at Burn Hall, Durham, in the 1780s, was not ideal. It was crescent-shaped and had a pavilion at each end, to provide storage space for hay. The cows were tied along the curve of the crescent and approached from a passage behind. The pavilions proved woefully impractical and had to be heightened, thereby losing the impact of the design.[4]

The building, nominally part of the farm, that appealed to architects most of all was the dairy. It soon became far from the utilitarian extension of the farmhouse that a proper working dairy had to be, and strayed into the province of Marie Antoinette's farmyard where she played at being a dairy-maid.[5] Soane's design for a dairy house 'in the Moresque style' (a published scheme, not a built one) included a tea room, dressing room and a cold bath. These glorified garden houses appear on numerous estates in forms which range from John Nash's thatched pill-box at Blaise Castle near Bristol to an almost oriental, nineteenth-century pavilion at Easton in Suffolk.

In fact, architecturally extravagant ideas for the farm had a short life in reality, as opposed to on paper, where they had a lengthy run. The lavish complex built in 1800 outside Workington in Cumberland by J. C. Curwen on the lines of an embattled medieval castle, complete with dummy moat and drawbridge, was a foible, not a pattern for the future. Similarly, the 'gentle-man's farm', which reached its most complete Palladian form in the 'hobby farms' outside Dublin, was a short-lived phenomenon which did not with-stand the harsh realities of the post-Napoleonic economic problems.[6] It did, however, influence the new farmhouse which began to turn away from the farmyard, literally and metaphorically.

Where the landscape was concerned in this period, it had to be both ornamental and productive. The extremes of the first requirement were reached with the idea that animals should graze the park land, as decoration, since they added to the liveliness of the scene. If possible a shepherd or cowman should be included. It was only a relatively short step to a time when the wife of a Victorian landlord in Dorset persuaded him to paint his home farm white and fill it with animals and poultry to match.

In fact, the ornamentation was just that. There might be a castellated folly at the end of a long avenue through the park, but the chances were that, as at Blenheim or Sledmere (in East Yorkshire), it disguised a farmhouse. The exception was the *ferme ornée* in which 'with the beauties which enliven a garden are everywhere intermixed many properties of a farm . . . even the clucking of poultry is not omitted.'[7] By the end of the eighteenth century that fad had passed. Humphry Repton, the landscape gardener, thought the idea was 'totally incongruous'. He continued, 'If the yeoman destroys his farm by making what is called a *ferme ornée* he will absurdly sacrifice his income to his pleasure.'

Despite everything, income was important and the financial incentives led some landlords to experiment on their home or park farms. From there tenants could take their cue; if the landowner was willing to experiment, then novel methods would be less baffling for the farmers elsewhere on the estate.

The improvements and innovations carried out on the home farms of the great estates, model farms in the sense that they were exemplary, were designed to be noticed. The eighteenth- or early nineteenth-century version was probably an architectural exercise but it was certainly also an agricultural one. Buildings and landscape could satisfactorily combine the façade of fashion with the function of utility. It was a short-lived revolution, however. The Napoleonic Wars had introduced a sense of unreality, with no foreign competition; at the resumption of peace everything was to change. As Cobbett recorded it, the post-Napoleonic depression was a crushing event for the small farmer – heavy taxation, competition from abroad and, in the rich lands of the southern counties, a big landowner standing in the wings ready to take over.[8]

In the meantime, the owners of large estates had been building up their fortunes. Innovation there in the late eighteenth century had been principally in layout. Where detail was concerned, however, it had included ingenious devices, such as Arthur Young's elaborate systems of subterranean pipes, hoists and cisterns, or his crane on wheels to unload waggons into the granary.

There were important pointers to the future in all this. Mechanization and mobility were just around the corner and it was only the hiatus of economic depression and political uncertainty between 1815 and the early 1830s that prevented their development much earlier. After all, tramways had been used in the mines in the seventeenth century and steam power was in use in Scotland and Staffordshire in the early nineteenth century.

Mechanization and mobility

On its foundation in 1838, the English Agricultural Society (soon to receive its Royal charter) gave among its objectives the encouragement of 'men of science in their attention to the importance of agricultural implements, the construction of farm buildings and cottages . . .'. Not everyone could keep up with the new pressures to mechanize and adapt. The *Journal of the Royal Agricultural Society* noted that where the new machines were concerned 'the farmer whose life is secluded has little opportunity to see them.' Even so, change was inevitably becoming increasingly swift. The mechanical reaper, first seen at the Great Exhibition in 1851, was much used by the 1870s, while later improvements, notably the combine harvester, were familiar sights within a few years of their first appearance.

The one place into which all these new aids would be absorbed eventually was the Victorian model farm. The men responsible for designing this more mechanized farmstead, expressive of 'high farming', were largely engineers and surveyors. Although there were exceptions, such as A. W. Pugin and Eden Nesfield, few Victorian architects tried their hand at farm buildings – if they did, they tended to be specialists in this particular field. When the earliest issues of the *Builder* began to publish designs for farm buildings in the 1840s, the authors bent over backwards to reassure the reader that these were sensible plans, thought up by men knowledgeable in agricultural matters and little concerned with aesthetic minutiae.

Changes to the Victorian farmstead were grafted on to the planned Hanoverian farmstead. Mechanization meant limited mobility (track systems were not all that flexible) and an increase in scale. The Victorian farmstead was also much affected by the new cheapness and availability of standardized

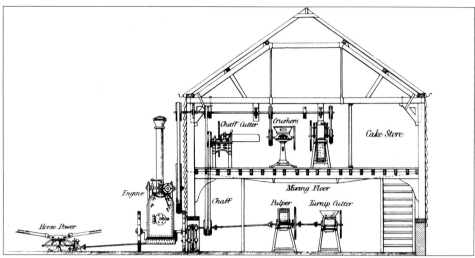

Above: The farmyard on wheels. From J. Bailey Denton's *Farm Homesteads of England* (1863). The rick is designed to be transported by a tramway system from rick yard to threshing barn. The engine house chimney can be seen behind denoting the source of power for threshing. The Victorian 'High Farming' lobby put much faith in technology of this type, although it was strictly only the province of highly capitalized and large-scale ventures.

Above right: The mechanical side of the mid-Victorian farm, illustrated by J. Bailey Denton. In this example, the horse-wheel seems to be shown as an auxiliary or used when the mobile engine is not available. No purpose built shelter is provided for the horse-wheel. Processing of foodstuffs was an important aspect of farming in an era of increasingly large livestock herds but before the advent of imported or ready-made fodder.

building materials. Taxes had been removed from bricks and tiles, iron manufacturers were producing catalogues of scores of useful components for the farmyard. By the 1870s, concrete had arrived, and was used at Robert Campbell's farm at Buscot in Berkshire and for cottages on the Gregynog estate in Powys. However, it was not yet a resounding success, having a tendency to 'sweat'.

Nevertheless, many farmers still depended on older buildings. There was much adaptation of vernacular farm buildings and J. C. Loudon's monumental encyclopaedia of the 1830s suggested farmers might alter 'mansions, Monasteries, Manufactures . . . so as to render them fit for agricultural purposes'.[9] For good measure, he also suggested a wide range of styles for a new farmstead – Grecian, Roman, Italian, Swiss, old-English cottage-style – any would do.

Loudon was also aware of the importance of mobility on the farm. Inspired by George III's famous 'ingenious moveable barn' at Windsor, he included advice on 'temporary, portable and ambulatory farmeries'. With the wider application of steam power and the expertise that had been developed with the railways, the farm could be developed on a system of tramlines along which trolleys could be trundled bearing the foodstuffs to the animals (or in some more fanciful instances, the animals to the foodstuffs). Anything, in principle at least, could be moved around this way. Such highly automated farms were not, in fact, very numerous; they were for the very rich landowner or the imaginative entrepreneur, and, as highly capitalized ventures, they were extremely vulnerable to changes in farming fortunes. Vast sums were spent on them and vast sums were lost. Such farms were theoretically, if less often in practice, a *tour de force* of imaginative engineering. One such bravura attempt was at East Harptree, near Bristol, where the buildings alone covered an acre and a half.

Building types: adaptation and new structures
On a practical level, most farms were changing gradually, as each category of

100

building was affected by the successive changes under the Agricultural Revolution and 'high farming'. Most writers of the late eighteenth century chided farmers for indulging in the construction of too many or too grandiose barns. But the relative loss of importance of the barn in the farming process was hard for them to comprehend – even for the progressive agriculturalists among their number. Barns had *always* been the heart of the farmstead. They had been second only to the house in the importance accorded to their construction and choice of materials. They had even shared the honours with the house in acquiring a dubious fashionable form – as follies in the landscape. Marshall dismissed the whole business: 'a barn dressed up in the habit of a country church or a farmhouse figuring away in the fierceness of a castle are ridiculous deceptions.'[10]

Barns still dictated the plan of the remodelled or new farmstead of the late eighteenth century but they were changing fast. In size, they were shrinking; only the doors grew larger, to allow in the bigger waggons now generally in use. However, the root house was expanding to store the increasing bulk of winter fodder for livestock; the barn was now subservient to the machinery which was beginning, in the early nineteenth century, to rule the farmstead.

As early as 1804, it was being claimed that mechanization, in the form of threshing machines, cut down on the need for buildings.[11] In many areas the horse- or water-power wheel stood outside, unprotected, but in the damper climates of the West and North it needed cover. There, the horse-wheel was housed in a circular or polygonal shed, usually tacked on to the back or side of an existing barn. The individual farmer's attitude to the new machinery depended much on the availability and cost of labour from area to area. In industrial regions, wages were much higher and so the threshing machine was far more enthusiastically embraced. Power might be provided by wind or water, but most probably by steam. The steam engine dictated its own structure, with a factory chimney – still a familiar feature of the Northumberland landscape. Here, as in Cornwall, industrial expertise passed between the local mines and the farm (sometimes in the hands of the same landowner).

The speed at which the corn crop was threshed and winnowed by threshing machine and fan meant that far more grain could be processed. This coincided with improved yields. The barn could not contain, nor was it convenient for it to do so, the vastly increased quantities produced on larger farms. It was used for all kinds of things: some storage, some processing of the root crops, and perhaps also for sheltering a few animals. Its clearly defined central role had, in some cases as early as 1800, already gone.

Storage
The increase in the amounts of straw (and hay, which was also responding to improved methods of husbandry) meant that other ways of storing the residue over winter had to be developed – more flexibility was needed than the traditional threshing barn provided. Temporary buildings were becoming more sophisticated. From the idea of thatching a lean-to shelter with bundles of straw, pea sticks, faggots or bracken (re-using the temporary roofing after it had served its use as thatch) evolved the idea of movable shelters, easily

demountable, and that of more flexible buildings – which could be re-erected elsewhere if necessary.

The Dutch barn was one such structure. Developed from a northern European prototype, it was first mentioned by Worlidge in the late seventeenth century: he called it a 'reek-staval' (or covered rick). It was, he said, much in use in the West Country. T. Lightholer's publication, *The Gentleman and Farmer's Architect* (1762), illustrates a Dutch barn, almost Chinese in character, with upturned eaves' ends. However, it was not widely adopted until the early nineteenth century. It gave a solid roof with good height to stacked hay or straw, which would otherwise have had to be thatched and carefully built around a central cone to aerate it. Although the commonest Dutch barn is the corrugated iron structure of the twentieth century, earlier versions were roofed in slate or tiles, and supported on pillars of stone, brick or slate, or on wooden posts. Later in the Victorian period, cast iron came in.

Rickyards, too, were an increasingly important feature of the late eighteenth- and nineteenth-century farmstead. They were rapidly superseding the barn, which had yielded its place as threshing became a mobile, mechanized process. As the yield, and often the acreage, increased on arable farms, it was necessary to stack the straw and this was done with care. The rickyards were thatched or even roofed, and stood on staddle stones, since in common with the contents of granaries, they were easy prey for mice.

The ricks were often constructed around a hollow cone to prevent them from overheating. In short, every care was taken to safeguard the important fodder store from predators; Burke took to task the careless farm servant who, by leaving his fork standing against a rick overnight, allowed access to rats, and rendered the staddle stones or coped pillars useless.

As the rickyard grew larger, the barn smaller and the quantities of corn greater, the granary became more important. It began to share the superior materials of house and barn, and in the early nineteenth century tended to have a noticeable profile with hipped roof, rising well above the height of the other buildings around the yard. This was the improved version of the granary, along with the detached version, supported on staddle stones, which had become well-established as a separate building type in the eighteenth century. Like the barn, and even more like the dairy, the granary tended to give free rein to the fantasies of those who were designing farmyards less for agriculture than for embellishment. Well into the nineteenth century, P. F. Robinson, wisely confining himself to the printed page, suggested a circular granary the outline of which 'would remind the traveller of the Temple of Venus in the Kingdom of Naples, on the coast of Baia, the roof assuming the form of the Temple of Vesta.'[12] Perhaps so.

Originally such roots as were grown seem to have been stored in any suitable dark corner – even the cellar of the farmhouse. With new schemes of rotation and a better understanding of fertilization, root crops became an increasingly important feature on the mixed farm and small specialized storage buildings were added to the farmstead accordingly. By the Victorian period the root house was considered to be an essential building in every well-designed model farm.

The demands of increased stock rearing

In the Victorian farm the main revolution lay in the shift from arable farming to that of intensive livestock rearing and fatstock breeding. The introduction of imported foodstuffs had improved the winter diet, allowing for much larger herds to be built up, and although grain was proving a losing market against foreign competition, meat was still relatively unchallenged (it did, however, arrive in tins from Australia in the 1860s). By the mid-nineteenth century, cattle were being fattened countrywide under intensive conditions redolent of modern 'battery beef'.

Open foldyards with surrounding shelter sheds were replaced by tied animals and covered sheds. These protected manure from dilution by rain and sun – according to the important evidence of Voelcker's experiments – as well as providing warmth for the beasts.[13] Yards multiplied. The animals needed light as well as warmth and soon windows were glazed as well as louvred – often half and half.

Hippolyte Taine visited a model farm in the 1860s. It consisted of a collection of fifteen or twenty low buildings, and the whole complex centred on livestock. The structures themselves 'were economically designed and built. Since the object was to put up a model, it would not have done to set the example of a costly edifice.' Bullocks, pigs and sheep were all being raised in airy, clean stalls. 'We were shown a system of byres in which the floor is a grating; beasts being fattened remain there for six weeks without moving.' The stock was valuable pedigree animals and there was even an Indian bull. Fodder was processed on the spot; chopped turnip, crushed beans and oil-cake were the winter fare and steam engines provided the power to treat it all. Some farms even had their own slaughter houses, using the refuse for fertilizer. A narrow-gauge railway moved it around the farmstead.

Silage was a late nineteenth-century improvement on the use of the grass crop. It was housed in purpose-built sheds or covered pits and provided a useful bulk foodstuff. On Lord Armstrong's progressive farm in Northumberland the pit still survives as a grain store. Another building that often formed part of the complex of farm buildings was the smithy; it was required for the maintenance of farm machinery as well as for shoeing the horses. There was plenty of work on a large farm to justify one, although smaller farms normally took advantage of the village blacksmith.

Just as the post-Napoleonic slump had followed the new dawn of the Agricultural Revolution, so a sequence of disastrous harvests and the arrival of tinned and chilled beef from the limitless expanse of South America, Canada and Australia tolled the bell for the end of 'high farming'. This time the crash was no temporary setback. Farming was not to recover from the Victorian failure to operate on a worldwide market before the onset of World War I. Then, as in the following war, enormous efforts were made towards agricultural self-sufficiency. Much labour was expended but no investment. Nothing had changed since the 1880s; a 1921 auction catalogue for a Devonshire estate near Torcross lists a wide range of specialized buildings which, with the exception of some 'galvanized iron' structures, show no sign of the age of Victorian 'high farming', let alone twentieth-century innovation.[14]

Left: Wheel-house (left of picture) and silo (centre) at a farm near Leatherhead, Surrey. Combinations of modern and traditional materials can sometimes be effective additions to the landscape.

Below left: Dutch barn of simple timber construction at a model farm at Eccleston, near Chester, on the Duke of Westminster's estate. Designed by John Douglas, the farm was part of a scheme for a village, built around 1875–80.

Below: Some modern buildings, like this grain store at Good Easter, Essex, complement the landscape, if well-sited. Despite being an 'off-the-peg' building, it has a smart, clean appearance which compares well with some other post-war agricultural buildings.

The tenant farmer

Adequate farm buildings mattered not only for the operation of the farm, they also played a crucial part in the relationship between tenant farmer and landowner. In lean years the buildings could be the inducement for new tenants; this had been the case as early as the 1730s and 1740s, and was so once again when farmers from the eastern farming counties of Scotland came down to take on some of the badly-hit East Anglian arable farms in the agricultural disaster years of the 1880s onwards. The tenant could make his own position more secure by dint of careful maintenance and by his own expenditure on the farmstead – dependent, of course, on outside circumstances. Bad times did not allow for new buildings – unless they were desperate measures. Many of the twentieth-century inter-war dairy farms could be classified under this category, for it was imperative for many farmers to change to dairy cattle, and new hygiene regulations and enlarged herds necessitated higher-standard cowsheds.

In the past a tenant could be frustrated by an agent (and, for that matter, *vice versa*). As intermediary, the agent, if indolent or inefficient, could fail to satisfy either landlord or farmer; on one of the Guy's Hospital estates in the late eighteenth century the buildings had fallen into a terrible state of disrepair, and the agent, William Fortune, was found to be at fault. His 'disposition was so trifling and neglects so frequent' that he was demoted.

The records for this estate give an interesting insight into this aspect of farm buildings. Between 1762 and 1815 'building and repairs' accounted for 9.5 per cent of expenditure from the gross income of the estate which, given the priority that the hospital had in claims for capital, was a high figure. Arrangements varied on estates; sometimes the tenant bore his own building and repair costs in exchange for commuted rent and a favourable lease. A good tenant was obviously in favour where there was a new or rebuilt farm to be allotted. Virtue in this matter generally went rewarded.

As the progressive Victorian farm kept in step with industrial development so too has the modern farm. The buildings of the 1960s and 1970s, like their predecessors of a century before, have not been hewn from the ground on which they stand, nor do their tools and power reflect their location. They are the most extreme stage in the gradual distancing of the buildings of the farm from the land on which they stand. Obviously the modern farmer has to be efficient; he also has to be careful. A good mixture of new buildings, well designed and sited, and the best possible use for the old ones is the ideal. It happens, but the happy examples of well-balanced groups are a negligible proportion of the total. Perhaps here, as in so many things, the constructive example of the past has something to convey to the future; unfortunately, it is a past all but forgotten.

The South East

Kent, Sussex and Surrey

These three south-eastern counties present a picture of neat, well-ordered farmland (the 'Garden of England', no less) but there are, in fact, a number of contrasting agricultural landscapes within this one small area. Apart from the trim and tidy Weald of Kent and Sussex, there are also the bleak marshlands of Kent, the heaths of Surrey and the large areas of cornland in all three counties. The low-lying coastal and river pastures have long supported fat cattle and sheep, whilst the downlands and rolling acres of West Sussex and East Kent respectively have sustained large-scale arable agriculture for centuries.

To a nineteenth-century eye such as Caird's, the small fields that had been cleared out of the forests covering the Weald of Kent and Sussex were anachronisms in an age of expansion and change; 'too much occupied by wood and cut up by overgrown hedges', he reported in disapproving tones. Nevertheless, the proximity to London, providing markets for both produce and a ready labour supply (both regular and seasonal), had given early prosperity to this distinctive area. Intensive husbandry developed in response to the small fields and existing woodland; fruit and hops flourished and the farm buildings reflected their special requirements.

The breakdown of the manorial system, already lapsed in many areas by the Tudor period, brought about a market in land and a burgeoning class of

Oast-house in a Wealden landscape.

106

yeoman farmers. These were the men who built and lived in the Wealden house, a sophisticated version of the medieval hall house, an elegant timber-framed structure suggesting the form of later farm-houses with its series of specialized domestic com-partments, defined by function. In their turn, the farmhouses gained from the higher standard of craftsmanship, both in the constructional methods of the master craftsmen and in the complex mixture of functions that could take place under the same roof.

The practice of gavelkind, where an inheritance was divided equally amongst the farmer's heirs, was held to have benefited agriculture in the South East. By contrast nineteenth-century observers con-sidered the local system of annual leases a burden that was leading to widespread fraud. Outgoing tenants could claim a sum in respect of draining, manuring and other improvements similarly hard to evaluate. Rascally valuers colluding with dishonest tenants compounded the problem, while tithes con-tinued to add to the burden of the law-abiding farmer. The Tithe Commutation Act was not passed until 1836 and did not remove the burden – merely its inconsistencies. From then on tithes were to be paid in cash, not kind, and the process was overseen by commissioners.

According to Caird, for example, farmers in the region combined 'a low scale of intelligence and small amount of capital and industry'. However, this view of Wealden practice was tainted by the Victorian idea that only intensive farming was worthy of note – hill farming was never mentioned in these accounts. To the seeker after improved agriculture, hill farming simply did not exist.

Although agricultural patterns were established early in the central areas of the three counties, the corn-growing areas – where the great religious houses had been responsible for both efficient agri-culture and buildings on a scale to match – were inevitably affected by the Agricultural Revolution, both in pattern and practice. The nature of farming around the edges of these south-eastern counties was altered by the amalgamation of holdings, pur-pose-built farmsteads and increasing sophistication in the combination of livestock and crops – improved sheep and corn husbandry, experiments with new root and fodder crops, elaborate rotation and mechanization all played their parts here as else-where. The marshes, too, drained and rendered more accessible with new roads, were to become more productive during the late eighteenth and early nineteenth centuries, as water-borne trans-port was no longer the only link between farm and market.

Building materials
Timber, particularly in the Weald of Kent and Sussex, was plentiful and, more important, of the highest quality. The expertise in carpentry in this area had been developed over centuries to such a point that the construction of timber-framed build-ings continued along much the same lines and to much the same standards into the eighteenth, or even early nineteenth, century. Marshall, writing in 1798, observed

> the fashion for *showy* farm-houses and offices has, fortunately perhaps, not yet gained a foot-ing here. The same style of buildings which has probably prevailed for centuries is yet, or has continued until very lately, in use.

Further 'the material of farm-building is still chiefly WOOD!' he exclaimed.

An important change affecting the local architec-ture was in the quality of the wood used in building. In 1790, oak cost 18d to 2s 6d per foot, beech a little less and elm about half that. By then, however, supplies of oak were running short, and the cheaper wood was far less durable.

In the Weald of Sussex, Marshall noted that 'splinters and shavings of hoops and other coppice wares' were being pressed into service for shingle roofing, albeit only for 'hovels and sheds'. Wattle, woven out of split oddments of timber, was bird-proof but animals sometimes ate it. Weather-board-ing was easier to construct and more practical.

Overleaf: Marden Thorn, near Staplehurst, Weald of Kent. The half-timbered farmhouse with its catslide roof, the weather-boarded barn with its hipped roof and the oasts make a harmonious blend of building materials, types and periods.

Right: Barn near Petworth. The tiling and weather-boarded walls are classic local techniques, arising from the abundant supply of raw materials, clay and wood, in this part of England.

However, thatch was still the popular roofing material for the outbuildings of the farm. But, when it came to the farmhouses, tiles were mostly used and by the nineteenth century they had virtually replaced thatch altogether. Thatch was, in fact, thought badly of by observers such as Marshall. He commented sternly, 'should this county continue to prosper and improve during the next century, as it has . . . the practice of covering farm buildings with the materials of manure will be wholly laid aside.' As an afterthought, he added that it was a fire hazard. Tiles, he noticed, were being used for walling as well as for roofing the domestic quarters. 'The modern shell is of ordinary studwork faced with flat tiles, put on scalewise, as slates are in the West of England.' Sometimes they were hung plain, and sometimes fancy shapes or patterns were introduced.

The oast house
Among the purpose-built structures of the farm, it is undoubtedly the oast house that conjures up the accepted image of Kent and Sussex; it provides a kind of icon for the region. The development of a specialized building for drying and packing hops was, in fact, proposed as early as the 1570s. The growing of hops was popularized by the Flemish weavers and Protestant emigrés from northern Europe during the Thirty Years' War, and the Weald suited the culture well; small fields and abundant timber for the hop poles were both available.

Oast houses came in many forms. There were some communal ones, although large growers sometimes had up to ten of their own (with additional warehousing for the pockets – the long canvas bags in which the hops were stored); yet in other areas, a single kiln might have been fitted into an existing barn. The required building had to house a kiln, fired originally by coke or charcoal, or indirectly by coal, so that the smoke did not taint the hops. Nowadays the process is powered by oil or electricity. An oast house had to be roomy, with a well-ventilated drying room, whitewashed to prevent condensation, and a slatted-floored cooling room, with horsehair matting over the slats. It also needed some kind of arrangement whereby the crop could be packed into the pockets. These various demands necessitated a vertical structure so that the filled pockets could arrive on the ground floor via a trap from the floor above, where they could be stored until collected or used. Rectangular kilns were the earliest type, followed by the characteristic, round oast house, which in turn was replaced in the nineteenth century by an improved rectangular type, which was easier to build. A cowl was developed to gain the maximum draught from the prevailing winds. For the few farmers still independently growing hops, the drying process is automated and the cowl is now redundant. Modern conversions of the oast house range from unappealing Georgianization, in which casement windows have been introduced at regular intervals up its height, to more careful adaptation to domestic and other uses which preserve the stark functionalism of the structure.

Hop and fruit cultivation
Fruit was widely cultivated when Celia Fiennes and Daniel Defoe made their observations on the landscape in this part of England. Fiennes noted a typical cherry orchard near Gravesend, which covered 'several acres of ground and runs quite down to the Thames, which is convenient for to convey the Cherries to London.' Labour for both these seasonal crops was plentiful. Wages in Kent were the highest in the country. Marshall observed the families who came to work with their children and noted the 'good humour and garrulity which is heard in every (hop) garden'. It was a sort of jubilee, 'during which a licence of speech and relaxation of manners are authorized by custom'. The tradition still continues, in fact, with the annual outings to the fruit orchards of Kent from the East End of London. Mechanization has, however, ended the hop-pickers' outings and 'pick your own' has changed the scene in the orchards.

Far left, above: farm at Highleadon, near Gloucester. The pierced brick nogging between the timbers is a typical ventilation device echoed in brick barns of a later date.

Far left: Farm near Chipping Norton, on the Oxfordshire/Warwickshire borders – an area of large farms of both manorial and later post-enclosure origins, in which mixed agriculture, often combining sheep with corn, has given rise to farm buildings which reflect the relationships between corn and livestock.

Although the fruit trees covered a considerable acreage, the fruit, once picked, was generally stored within a barn, or even in the farmhouse. The extensive fruit-growing occasioned no purpose-built structures – the requirements for it were simply for well-ventilated, dry and vermin-proof quarters.

The barns

In East Sussex, many hundreds of multi-purpose timber-framed barns still survive today. Across the region as a whole there must be a remarkably high count. Just as the north German barn is covered by an all-embracing roof which simply alters pitch to encompass the width, these 'mere tents', as Marshall termed the English ones, have a roof

> which is brought down to within a few feet of the ground; in order to provide stabling, cattle sheds, lodgements for implements, straw etc, and, of course, vermin; of which those lean-tos or 'killases' are the nurseries and harbours.

Hops, fruit, wool (many farmers combined agriculture with employment in the woollen trade, in mining or in forestry) and even the labourers themselves were accommodated under this one roof. Perhaps this economy was not altogether a success for, as Marshall pointed out, the labourers showed 'a want of alertness . . . probably caught from the sluggish animals they have been enured to work with'.

In the arable farming areas of the region, the timber-framed barns, large and small, were aisled. Generally, if they were more than five bays in length, they had two threshing floors; if less, a single one.

The farmstead

As far as the general pattern of the farmstead is concerned, the arable part of this region has much in common with the East Anglian corn-growing counties, while the downs of West Sussex mirror

Typical group of red-tiled, brick-nogged and timber-framed farm buildings, with tarred weather-boarding, near Wisborough Green in West Sussex. The bricks and tiles are of Wealden clay, the timber locally grown.

Right: Plum picking near Faversham, Kent. Londoners over the centuries have come to the Kentish fruit fields – the radio and truck add the only touches of modernity.

Far right: A hop garden near Marden in Kent, 'one of many fine hoppe yards', as Celia Fiennes described them in the 1690s. Few farmers these days grow hops independently, since most hop gardens are the property of the big brewing companies; only about 100 farmers in the Weald of Kent and Sussex carry on the tradition.

the practices of the adjacent counties of the South-West. Barns, granaries and large-scale cattle accommodation showed little variation on standard buildings of the southern counties. Pigs, which had previously taken pannage from the spinneys and hedgerows, were housed, or at least enclosed, in fields. Some coastal areas were adapted to arable husbandry after the post-Restoration Corn Bounties made corn-growing more attractive than the rearing of livestock. Nevertheless, cattle came on hoof and by water from the North and from Wales to be fattened on pastures close to London, and sheep were important in this area both for wool and mutton.

The modern farming scene

Today, the picture is not so very different from that of Marshall's day. The distinctive buildings – the Wealden farmhouse and the timber-framed, aisled barns of the corn-growing regions of Kent and the smaller multi-purpose barns of East Sussex and Surrey – still dot, and even define, the landscape. The later additions, the cowl-topped oast houses of the hop-growing areas or the large-scale downland farms, built by improving landlords and agents on the great estates, exist today – even if put to other uses.

This part of England, wealthy in the past, is still characterized by an air of comfort and prosperity, echoed in the warm tones of the buildings, and in their compact forms and the softness of the weathered wood and clay. Although stockbrokers and solicitors may sally forth from the farmhouses and from the disused oast houses, the picture, if not the purpose, remains intact.

However, the greatest threat to agriculture in the south-eastern counties has been that of urban encroachment. The introduction of Green Belt legislation in 1947 belatedly safeguarded the remnants of the most vulnerable areas but elsewhere expansion, and subsequent inflationary land values, has made the livelihood of the smaller independent farmer once again a precarious business.

Right: A characteristic set of buildings for a mixed Wealden farm at Staplehurst, Kent. The gallery leads to a cooling room in the oast house where the hops are put into 'pockets' or long sacks. The wooden hurdles around the cattle yard denote a well-wooded locality, a principal factor in determining the growth of hops, as there was a ready supply of hop poles.

Below: Distant view of the Wealden house at Edenbridge, Kent, shown on page 53, seen here with its neighbouring oast houses. The cooling area is between the two kilns.

Left: A fine 18th-century granary with Dutch gables and high-quality glazing at a farm at Chart Sutton, near Staplehurst, Kent. Gables like these are more familiar in Norfolk, but were also adopted in the coastal counties of south-east England from the late 17th century.

Below: An apple orchard at the same farm.

Farm near Smarden, Kent. The weather-boarded double-pile farmhouse has neat hipped roofs. The oast (with its cowl gone) is comparable to other examples shown earlier but has a roof extension, possibly to accommodate later machinery.

Left: A modern timber cattle shed, West Sussex.

Top: A 20th-century oast near Tenterden, Kent.

Above: A 19th-century wheel-house near Leatherhead, Surrey.

The Cotswolds and Southern Counties

Dorset, Wiltshire, Avon, Gloucestershire, Oxfordshire, South Buckinghamshire (the Chilterns), Berkshire, Hampshire.

In this region, the most marked agricultural contrasts lie between the agriculture of the downs and hill-tops – chalk or stone areas devoted to sheep and corn husbandry – and that of the broad, rich valleys of the region, traditionally well suited to dairying. In the chalk or stone areas, farms have tended to be larger, since the land has been poorer, but many holdings combine both rich and poor land, and so mixed farming has been possible.

These contrasts in landscape are naturally reflected in the materials of the buildings. Where the Jurassic limestone belt runs, from Dorset in the south on a north-easterly line through the Cotswolds, the buildings are cream, grey or golden – crisply built and often elegantly detailed. The landscape itself is strong, but not harsh; the farmsteads seem to treat it with respect and only the field barns stand isolated. To the east of that line, where chalk has provided the raw materials, the buildings become softer. Dug rather than quarried from the earth, the materials, cob, clunch and flints, produced thick walls nestling under giant roofs, with their overhanging thatched eaves. Further east again, and to the south, the timber and brick are reminders of the connections with the adjacent counties. In the south of this region, thatch was widespread and much remains today. Thatched cob walls are a particular feature, with the eaves usefully preventing the earth-based cob

Flint and brick in the Dorset downlands.

124

wall from disintegration in wet conditions. Elsewhere stone and clay tiles have been used for roofing and, with the advent of the canals, slate.

At the south-eastern extremity of the area, Hampshire provides a meeting point for the two types of timber-framing which are dominant in the south-eastern and western counties respectively, box-framing and cruck construction (though the latter is something of a rarity). This county also has examples of the Wealden house and an abundance of good timber and heavy clays led to a tradition of skilfully constructed brick-nogged panels on the farmhouses and barns. The weather-boarding, timber-framing and flintwork, now so valued in the landscape, had little value in the eyes of the industrious entrepreneurs of Victorian farming. In the nineteenth century some of the 'wretched old wood and thatch hovels common in the country' were replaced here as elsewhere with factory-made bricks and blue slates.

Mixed farming: the barn

On the downlands of Dorset, Wiltshire, Hampshire and Berkshire, and on the exposed hillsides of the Cotswolds – between them a considerable proportion of this area – the agriculture had, and still has, much in common with the Lincolnshire and Yorkshire Wolds. The dominant sheep and corn husbandry – corn on the hill-tops, pastures in the dry valleys, and the sheep moved between the two – attracted the notice of that acute traveller, Celia Fiennes. Passing near Salisbury she observed, 'this country is most champion and open, pleasant for recreations; its husbandry is mostly corn and sheep . . . the little towns or villages lie in the valleys.' Later on, Thomas Hardy immortalized the open downlands of Dorset in *Tess of the d'Urbervilles*. He

A fine early 16th-century barn at Grange Farm, Basing, Hampshire, recently restored. The weather-boarded granary, supported on staddle stones, right, is on the same farm. It is one of many such granaries in this part of southern England.

described 'fields so large as to give an unenclosed character to the landscape, the lanes are white, the hedges low and plushed, and the atmosphere colourless'.

Long before, great medieval landowners (among them the colleges of the new university at Oxford) had run their huge flocks of sheep over the thin pastures and had farmed vast acreages of corn. They and the other, mainly ecclesiastical, land-owners had constructed the great tithe barns to receive these crops. Unlike other buildings of that period they still stand today.

The stone-built tithe barns, masking fine, timber-framed interiors, are one of the architectural glories of this part of the country. To the south, in the Chilterns, Berkshire and Hampshire, the later barns incorporate brick with the timbering, recording a prosperity based on corn.

Long after the medieval period, both the barns and the sturdy manorial farmhouses retained the features of Gothic architecture: gables, mullions and quatrefoil or trefoil decoration. On barns the latter were sometimes put to utilitarian use for ventilation and, incidentally, as an entrance for owls, who were encouraged to kill vermin the barns.

Marshall was rather disparaging about the vast dimensions of the Cotswold barns; 'one foot below the beams is worth two above', he commented, inferring that their dimensions were rather more for show than for practical purposes.

Nevertheless, better returns and bigger acreages required more barns and bigger stables. Much of this extra space was realized in the eighteenth century by the adaptation and enlargement of existing buildings, rather than the wholesale rebuilding of farmsteads. The quality of construction of the buildings in both stone and brick districts had ensured their survival, unlike other areas further west or north.

The granary

Another outcome of the pressure on the eighteenth-century farmstead to expand its provision for arable farming was the emphasis placed on adequate granaries. Marshall observed that granaries were being incorporated into the upper regions of barns by the insertion of a floor above the pitched

entrance porches. With this plan, corn could be lifted up with a tackle to be stored until it was needed and then shot down into bags below.

Alternatively, the granary could be incorporated as a room above the stables or cart-shed, approached by a separate outside stair, and well secured. Most commonly, however, granaries were timber-framed structures, supported on staddle stones. The brick-panelled granary of this type is very typical of the eastern district of this region (although it also appears in the limestone regions) and there are an estimated 250 or more of these in Hampshire alone. Later granaries became even larger, virtually extra-secure barns in fact. Since both barns and granaries were often sited in the valleys where rats were a particular menace, brick plinths or staddle stones were essential to protect the grain.

Sheep and cattle

Sheep here as elsewhere needed little more than a system of hurdles and perhaps a demountable shelter for exposed sites. Cattle, however, had buildings, but poor ones. Caird noticed the discrepancy in Hampshire between the huge barn and the inadequate cattle sheds 'entirely without plan or convenience either of labour or food'. However, cattle were, even in the nineteenth century, a secondary consideration in the sheep- and corn-based husbandry. Caird found plenty of cattle being fattened along the river banks of Wiltshire but pointed out that in the Cotswolds the evidence of management for beef-rearing

> leads us to infer that cattle do not form a very important item in the profits of Cotswold farming. The stock were all tied up in open sheds, thus exposed to the wind, without the power of changing their position. Their provender was a mixture of hay and straw cut into chaff by a machine driven by horse-power.

Where livestock was concerned, this part of the country seemed more advanced in respect to fattening pigs and sheep; the latter, 'store-sheep', were housed in Oxfordshire in generous yards 'surrounded with warm sheds, cheaply constructed with hurdles, and roofed with loose straw'. Despite such care, Caird's observation was that 'the land-lords of this county interest themselves very little in agriculture'.

The lush valleys and vales of the southern counties were for dairy cattle. Here the importance of the riverside pastures dictated the sites for the farmsteads, and they can be found spaced out along the valleys of Wiltshire and the Vale of Gloucester for example. The farmhouse here incorporated dairies and often cheese stores as well. The dairy herds were implied in Marshall's summing up of the Vale of Amesbury: 'a most desirable county to farm in. Sound sheep walks; arable lands, that may be worked in almost any season; meadowy valleys and calcareous water.'

Poverty and wealth

Historically, the southern part of this region was not always kind to its farmers. Common land had been desperately over-stocked and, with enclosure, there was a vast demand by the enormous numbers of landless labourers for the remnants of unenclosed land. Destitution became widespread; the work-houses filled with country people who could no longer survive in the outside world.

There were plans for land-based communities, one of the first of which had been Defoe's scheme for German refugees in the New Forest. That, like many, came to nothing. Even those few that were set up could make little impression on the scale of destitution that Cobbett recorded on his travels shortly after the end of the Napoleonic Wars. Many small farmers, in Dorset for example, did not weather the post-Napoleonic crisis years. Unfavourable grain and land prices conspired against them. Independent rather than tenant farmers, they did not have the security of the land-owner's wealth, and large estates therefore expanded at the expense of these small farmers. Where the big landowner built a farm, he sited it near a water point or dug a well. New upland farms in these counties are usually well screened by tree planting.

Although Cobbett was horrified by the parlous state of much of the agriculture in this region, he was nevertheless occasionally impressed. In particular, he recorded Lord Folkestone's efforts at Coleshill in Berkshire, where the steward, Mr Palmer, had built up 'the most complete farm-yard that I ever saw' where 'all are comfortable; gaunt hunger here stares no man in the face.' There was a stall full of oxen 'and they are all fat, how it would make a *French* farmer stare!' Cobbett found this farm in direct contrast to the situation nearby at Cricklade where the produce of the fine dairy pastures was conveyed away by canal, while the poverty-stricken men and women and their families consumed a meagre diet based on potatoes. 'Was it not better for the consumers of the food to live near to the place where it was grown?' he suggested.

Improvements in agriculture

The eastern counties of this group were clearly favourite areas for agricultural experiment, especially in the Victorian 'high farming' era. The high quality land, easy terrain and proximity to markets earmarked Hampshire and Berkshire, in particular, as good areas in which to invest in land and in which to experiment with new and im-proved methods of farming. One example was in Berkshire, where Robert 'Tertius' Campbell had produced an ingenious sugar beet liquor-extrac-tion plant at Buscot. In this way, he combined the fattening of cattle with the production of sugar beet, a cost-effective partnership rather similar to the corn and sheep husbandry. Despite the domi-nance of sheep, corn and dairy farming, the fashion for fatstock in Victorian farming did not miss the other southern counties entirely. Many of the large hereditary landowners were building model live-stock farms – at Wilton and Longleat in Wiltshire, for instance. Marshall had already seen bullocks being fattened in individual stalls and yards at the end of the eighteenth century near Gloucester.

In the 1850s, on a progressive farm in Berkshire, both pigs and sheep were being fattened under cover, standing on slatted floors through which the manure fell on to the prepared chaff below – thus instantly providing manure ready for the fields; a sophisticated arrangement for its time.

Despite the general impression of large-scale enclosure and engrossing, and the weak position of the small independent farmer-proprietor, there have been remarkable survivals of earlier farms amidst the change. One farm at Compton Beauchamp, on the Berkshire Downs, had preserved until 1930 the boundaries of a holding document in a charter of AD 903 and the farmstead still stood within the protection of the moat.

The picture today

Modern farming has made a very visible impression on farming in the arable areas of the southern and south-central counties. The corn bins, grain dryers, silage equipment, enormous cattle sheds and milking parlours give an accurate idea of the increase in scale of farming over the last couple of decades. Sometimes institutional investors have replaced the great private landowners of the nineteenth century. Probably the majority of those larger barns still standing remain in some kind of agricultural use – however irksome they may be to the farmer or landowner. As ever, it is the outlying cattle-sheds and foldyard, the field barn or the tiny shepherd's shelter hut that are inevitably redundant – sadly now the obsolescent face of tradition.

Right: A 17th-century farmhouse at West Yatton, Wiltshire – the mullioned windows and stone tiles are original features. The catslide roof, behind, covers the former service area.

Top: Farmhouse at Sandford St. Martin, Oxfordshire. The three left-hand bays date from the 16th century and have mullioned windows with square hoods. The three right-hand bays are of early 18th-century construction. The farm buildings follow the lie of the road, and the farmyard is entered through the double doorway in the barn.

Above: Cotswold stone has been used for a range of traditional farm buildings at Didbrook in Gloucestershire – the complex roofscape is a regional feature.

Below: A traditional cart-shed houses modern equipment at a farm near Blandford, Dorset. The gentle curve of the corn thatch emphasizes the attractive lines of the building. The farm and its buildings are grouped close to the parish church, forming a typical manorial group.

Above: Open-fronted cattle sheds at West Yatton, Wiltshire. The tubby columns are characteristic of the stone building traditions of this part of the country.

Below: Similarly open-fronted cattle sheds, but of a later date and a rather different design. These 19th-century shelter sheds at Stalls Farm, Longleat in Wiltshire were built for the Marquis of Bath as part of a carefully planned architect-designed farmstead. A drawing and plan of the farm are shown on page 28.

A stone-built farm at West Kington in Wiltshire. Neat symmetrical farmhouses, barns and shelter sheds are familiar features in the Wiltshire landscape – a rich agricultural area.

Right: Farm implements in a stone and timber barn at Hill Deverill, Wiltshire.

Opposite: The manorial farmhouse and generously sized farm pond at Stert in Wiltshire.

136

The South West

Devon, Cornwall, Somerset and Avon

There are two agricultural landscapes in this region which remain as obvious and as separate in the late twentieth century as they were to travellers recording the scene 300 years ago. Daniel Defoe noted this; Exmoor, for example, was barren ground 'but as soon as the Ex comes off from the moors and hilly country, and descends into the lower grounds, we found the alteration; for then we saw Devonshire in its other countenance, viz. cultivated, populous and fruitful.' In other words the harsh, inhospitable moorland beat off all but the most marginal kinds of agriculture, as the farmer scraped a living by combining the scant, upland grazing with the slightly more nourishing pastures on the moor edge to provide sustenance for sheep and cattle. At the other extreme, the lush landscape of much of the rest of this western peninsula, with its maritime climate, allowed for a rich pastoral economy. In the wide valleys of the principal rivers, cornlands supplemented these two livestock-based forms of livelihood.

Upland farming takes place amidst a sternly beautiful landscape, its grey granite farmsteads scattered within hamlets or occasionally closer to the moor edge. In the lowland pastures, verdant the year round, stone or cob farms dot the countryside, often quite alone, sometimes set into the village street. Here and there glowing red fields emerge, echoed in the red cob buildings. Fields

Barton near Kingsbridge, Devon.

138

tend to be small and bounded by banked-up soil and thick hedges, or by overgrown stone walls. Cattle are everywhere – in Devon a richly red breed, at one with soil and buildings.

It is the cattle that provide the links between the upland and lowland farming. On the edges of Dartmoor, Exmoor or Bodmin Moor, the farm usually straddles the line between two kinds of grazing – often situated precisely on the line that separates the harder and softer soil, and thus where a spring emerges. These farmsteads, granite-walled and slate-roofed, merging into the bleak scenery, are designed above all to provide shelter from the rough climate. Heavy walls and enclosed yards are essential, together with foundations dug well into the hillside. Roughcast, a mixture of lime and gravel, sometimes elaborated to give the impression of stonework, was a traditional finish, as were slates, hung vertically on the end wall of the farmhouse. Insulation and impermeable surfaces were of paramount importance for the farmer and his family, as well as for his livestock, when they came under cover.

The lowland farmer also chose to live near a natural water source where possible. Early farm sites in the West Country are often about a third of the way up a valley side, since the bottom is too damp and holds the frequent mists, and the top is too exposed. Sometimes the farm is at the head of a coomb or dell. These ancient sites are proof, along with the field patterns or even the actual hedges or walls, of pre-Domesday farming, if not Iron or Bronze Age cultivation.

Agricultural patterns of the region

In 1382 it was stated that farmers of the region had cultivated the land 'from times where memory is not'. There are many clues to support the claim of the western counties to have established the earliest stable agricultural pattern. Since much of the farmland lay within easy reach of the ports, a thriving trade in victualling ships had grown up by the end of Elizabeth I's reign, and increasing prosperity enhanced the agricultural stability.

Opposite, above: Farms like this one at Morvah, Cornwall, may well have Celtic origins.

Opposite: Mounting block outside a farmhouse at Altarnun, Cornwall, c. 1585.

Remoteness from sources of invasion or political unrest has its advantages, as can be seen by contrasting this area with Northumberland, for example, which was vulnerable on both these counts until well into the eighteenth century, so that much of its agricultural and rural landscape dates only from the nineteenth century.

The landholding patterns were established early, divided between the 'bartons' (from 'bere', meaning barley, and 'ton', a stockade) – originally demesne, or manorial, lands – and a large class of prosperous independent freeholders; later reorganization brought about by enclosure largely passed the West Country by. Marshall, who was himself improving the farm at Buckland in Devon, commented on the various kinds of farmer; the family farm in which 'the farmer, his wife, sons and daughters do much of the labour themselves' has probably changed remarkably little since his comments were published in the late eighteenth century. Marshall had little use for tradition, however; and he commented that on such farms the 'spirit of improvement [was] deeply buried under an accumulation of custom and prejudice.' The landed gentry were little better: 'Men of landed property, it might be said, have lately been slumbering on their own concerns, and dreaming about the business of their tenants.' He did find one race to praise. In the South Hams district in south Devon (then, as now, one of the principal corn-growing areas) are 'small farmers, men who think for themselves and act without the authority of their ancestors'.

Farmhouse and buildings

Where the farmhouse was concerned, the usual distinctions between upland and lowland patterns applied. In lowland areas, the house frequently long outlived the other farm buildings and is therefore of different materials and construction; so the two sectors, farmhouse and 'farmery', are well separated. In the highland areas, the longhouse plan was favoured, combining domestic and animal quarters under one sloping roof-line, each with a separate access. The shippon was built on the lower end of the slope, a practical arrangement in which drainage took place as far as possible

unaided, the flagged floor having a central drain leading to a dung pit or midden. It was not unusual for the other buildings of the farmstead (if there were any) to conform to the lowland pattern with a south-facing barn and a sheltered yard. Generally there were fewer buildings than in the lowland counterpart, reflecting smaller holdings and less diversity. Sheep were kept but did not require substantial cover – hurdles and stout walls generally sufficed.

The climate allied to the different farming habits produced a number of localized building types or, at least, regional modifications to better-known elements within the farmstead. The variously named 'linhay' or 'linney' is one such. An adaptation of a shippon, it was thus described by Caird:

> the back walls being built close up to the eaves; the front is in two storeys, supported on strong posts of timber open from the ground to the eaves, the lower storey occupied by cattle, the upper kept as a store for their provender.

That, more or less, is the standard linhay of Devon – though the supports may be rough stone columns or even great slate slabs. Marshall describes them as sometimes being built back-to-back, which seems odd since the open-fronted loft or 'tallet' was designed to give maximum exposure to the sun and drying winds. Sometimes it was screened by weather-boarding. The back wall was stoutly built to withstand cold and northerly winds, perhaps thick enough to incorporate a few nesting places for pigeons. The tallet would be reached by ladder, sometimes inside, sometimes outside, and the hay was pushed down from there through an aperture in the floor into the racks below.

Around Bridgwater, Defoe noticed, 'this country is all a grazing, rich, feeding soil.' Frequent flooding helped to keep it so. In these rich cattle lands, which include the Somerset Levels (the West Country equivalent of the eastern fenlands), cattle are housed in buildings roofed with pantiles. The same argument applies here; the natural ventilation provided by these heavy ridged tiles (which also provide insulation) has no modern competition.

Cattle determined the form of many types of West Country farm. The farm centred on the fold-yard, and precious midden, where the cattle gathered – sometimes with lean-to protection from the worst of the climate. A bull pen, calf boxes and a shippon for oxen might make up one side of the yard, whilst the linhay, stabling and cart-sheds enclosed a further two sides. Generally the fourth was open, though an entrance below a granary into a closed yard was a Devon feature.

On dairy farms the production of butter and cheese required their own facilities – though these were generally provided within the farmhouse and varied little from region to region. Defoe describes the cheese-making at Cheddar, a lively communal undertaking ('the whole village are cowkeepers') with the cows feeding on well-manured common-land. However, until the late nineteenth century most cheese was produced on individual farms.

A record of a south Devon farm in 1606, with seventy-two acres, lists a great diversity of buildings in the farmstead, reflecting the range of activities on a farm. There was a cow-house and a milkhouse, a barn, stable, shippon, workshop, larder-house, bake-house and cider-house. Both Celia Fiennes and Defoe commented on the volume of cider production in Somerset and south Devon. Tens of thousands of hogsheads full of cider left the area each year for London. The apple-mill had been invented in 1664, which allowed animal power (normally donkeys) to be harnessed for the manufacture of cider. A simple rectangular building, the pound-house, was developed to house the process, though only on larger farms. As Marshall observed, it often took place in a 'mean shed or hovel, without peculiarity of form or any trace of contrivance'. The purpose-built structure took the line of a gentle slope, with loose fruit being placed at the upper end, carried by a spout to the mill or press below and from there to a lower ground floor fermenting room. Cider-making has gone, with few exceptions, to the factory – along with cheese-making. But the orchards remain an important feature of the Somerset landscape, providing sheltered grazing for sheep and, when in blossom, foaming from horizon to horizon like some unsettled sea.

Right: Farm near Zennor, Cornwall. The farm site marks the border between the rough grazing above and the more fertile lower pastures. The farmhouse and buildings have been sited to take advantage of the change of level, and shelter from the prevailing winds.

Below: Valley farm in the Brendon Hills, Somerset. The area is part of the Exmoor National Park.

The dimensions and importance of the barn in the West Country reflect the nature of the agriculture. In the corn-growing valleys such as Taunton Vale (known as 'the Paradise of England' in the early 1600s because of its fertility), the barns were commensurately large. Wheat surplus was shipped to London from both Devon and Somerset, though not from Cornwall, although wheat was grown there too. In fact, Cornwall tended to surprise visitors, being less harsh than they imagined; but, as Defoe put it,

> though it is fruitful enough for the supply of its own inhabitants yet, in the first place, the waste grounds are so many, the inhabitants so numerous and the county so narrow . . . they have not much overplus to furnish other parts with.

Marshall merely remarked that he was surprised to find things 'not too wretched'.

The remoteness of many West Country farms meant that they have always had to be exceptionally well provided with storage space – with more than might seem necessary. Hay was valuable winter fodder, sometimes having to stretch a winter that lasted until April. A building both dry and properly ventilated was imperative, otherwise the precious sustenance rotted and the animals had to be prematurely slaughtered.

In Devon and Cornwall the two-level barn was constructed on the northern pattern, utilizing the lie of the land to allow hay to be stored at one level, with animals or more often a threshing floor and further storage below. Folding doors and a good roof overhang were precautions against driving winds and heavy rainfall gusting in. Elsewhere, conventional corn barns are to be found, constructed from local materials and as large as the acreage demanded. To the east of the area there was a number of great tithe barns, such as the one at Buckland Abbey, which Marshall personally adapted for eighteenth-century waggons by knocking a new entrance through the great stone walls. Previously, crops had been carried in by horses loaded with sacks or panniers. The barns of each area, cob-walled and thatched in south Devon, of red sandstone around Exmoor, and of dark slate and stone in much of Cornwall, provide an idea of the range of materials within the region. Further variations, such as between reed and straw thatch, one type of sandstone or another, intensify the differences.

Mechanization of the Cornish tin mines and china clay works in the nineteenth century led to the sharing of skills and the introduction of the wheel-house, the distinguishing feature on the Cornish farmstead – although the innovation soon spread into Devon. As in the North East, mining techniques aided the development of mechanized farming and both horse-wheel and engine-house were adopted in Cornwall long before they were taken up by many other ostensibly more progressive and prosperous agricultural regions.

The sturdy traditional buildings of the West Country farmstead still serve their purpose remarkably well, especially compared to flimsier modern equivalents. One farmer enthusiastically described to me the advantages of keeping his calves and cattle over winter in a traditional linhay. Unlike many of his neighbours' animals, his own remain free of pneumonia – the result, he claims, of the advantage of the natural materials (timber, stone and cob) over inadequate modern substitutes, particularly asbestos, in which condensation builds up alarmingly. Some recent winters, such as that of 1978–79, served to remind the non-agricultural world that life in remote regions still contains its share of hardships, which have hardly lessened over the centuries. Sheep still have to be dragged free of snow drifts, and milk has to be flushed away if the tanker cannot get to the farm. It may be cosier in the modern farmhouse in front of the television but outside, on the hills, farming is still tough.

Overleaf: A large and solid farmhouse in the Forest of Dean, Gloucestershire. In the 16th and 17th centuries many of the farms here were squatter holdings, with the farmers not only cultivating the land, but working part-time as iron-smelters as well; the thickly wooded valleys provided ample fuel for the charcoal furnaces.

Right: Dartmoor landscape, showing signs of enclosure, probably of the late 18th, early 19th century. The walls mark the boundaries of an individual farmer's property, and offer much needed shelter for animals. The climate of Dartmoor is not only often harsh, but highly variable, with little natural protection.

Left: Farm at St. Erth, Cornwall, an area where many farm sites are of great antiquity. The glazed windows denote either the granary or possible accommodation for farm servants. A few perches for doves are pierced into the stonework.

Right: A solid 18th-century farmhouse near St. Erth, Cornwall. The whitewash has been applied over random stonework.

Below: Massive range of farm buildings at Roscarrock, Cornwall.

Right: A barton (the Devon term for a farmyard) at Tamerton Foliot, Devon. A road running through the centre of a farm may denote an irregular pattern of land-holding, more frequent in western counties.

Below: A cob-walled thatched barn in the Otter Valley, south Devon. The pinky-red soil used as a building material gives homogeneity to buildings and landscape in this area.

Bottom left: A round-house (the Devon name for a wheel-house) in the Otter Valley. Both horse and wheel were under cover; the sides (now weather-boarded) would have been open, and the threshing machine would have been in the barn attached.

150

Right: A slab of granite serves as a gatepost in north Devon.

Below: Devon linhay in the Otter Valley. The open-fronted loft allows wind and sun to dry the hay, which will not otherwise dry completely in the fields, owing to the damp climate. Some linhays are closed on the ground level, some open. Adaptations of this type are found in other damp western regions.

Above: A farm on the edge of
the Quantock Hills in Somerset.
The 18th-century farmhouse
has a relatively small barn –
typical of a predominantly
pastoral area.

Left: Open shelter sheds at a
manorial farm, next to the
church, at East Quantoxhead,
Somerset. To the right is a
barn, its back wall used to
enclose the sheds and to the left
is a thatched cart-shed.

Right: Farm on the edge of the
Quantock Hills, looking towards
Exmoor in the far distance.
Grazing on the hillsides and
arable land in the valleys is the
usual pattern in regions where
upland and lowland conditions
are found together, as here.

The Eastern Counties

Essex, Norfolk, Suffolk, Cambridgeshire, Bedfordshire, Hertfordshire.

The flat, dry expanse of the eastern counties of England has long lent itself to the practice of large-scale arable farming. Suitability of terrain and climate, proximity to major markets and relative ease of communication have all worked in its favour. If you add to that the historical accident which found 'Turnip' Townshend, Coke of Norfolk and Arthur Young revolutionizing agriculture in the counties of Norfolk and Suffolk, and the independence of spirit noted in its people, it becomes obvious that the area possessed all the ingredients for progress and innovation.

The absence of a manorial tradition in a considerable part of this region no doubt helped to foster independent experiment. Yeoman farmers, who sometimes lived in some style in former manor houses, were growing root crops, such as turnips and carrots, as early as the beginning of the seventeenth century, and were also breeding pigs and turkeys intensively – as they do today.

The deficiencies in the soil that might have discouraged less enterprising farmers merely caused the Hertfordshire farmer, for example, to import vast quantities of London manure; and he put it to such good use that, in the eighteenth century, grain described as coming from that county (often falsely) commanded a higher price than any other.

Equally, the limitations of the soil and terrain in the fenland areas of Cambridgeshire merely served

The early 13th-century Wheat and Barley barns (left and right respectively) at Cressing Temple, Essex.

154

to encourage initiative: this time in the shape of a massive drainage scheme carried out in the seventeenth century. It was undertaken from 1630 onwards by the Duke of Bedford and his company of 'Adventurers and Undertakers', on the basis that those who risked money in the venture would be rewarded with an allotment of the newly drained land. Despite terrible set-backs and interruptions the scheme was eventually successful. These early efforts in enterprise set the scene for the great developments in agricultural practice that took place from the eighteenth century onwards. Not for nothing was it suggested in an essay, published in 1804, that landowners should 'transplant into each district a few tenants from situations where the management of stock and the improvement of meadow and pasture lands are better understood'. The situations referred to were, of course, Norfolk and Suffolk. This part of the country was so much in advance of other regions that even the farm labourers were thought to be a superior group: unlike their counterparts in Kent they were reputed to be 'active and generally brisk about their tasks'.

Forms of agriculture

No doubt because of its reputation, the agriculture of this region has been well recorded. A number of the records stem from foreign visitors in the eighteenth century, but even as far back as the sixteenth century Thomas Tusser of Essex had recorded his percipient observations on the physical nature and social habits of England. By the eighteenth century, when François, Duc de la Rochefoucauld, and Pehr Kalm of Sweden visited the area, the revolution in farming methods was well under way.

Below: The Swaffham and Bottisham Engine Drain of 1821, Swaffham Prior, Cambridgeshire, in the fenland landscape – a triumph of 19th-century engineering.

Right: Chalky landscape near Sandon in Hertfordshire – similar to many other downlands in the country. The track has probably preserved the line of an ancient route.

But to some foreign eyes the progress of enclosure and the neatness of the landscape, while impressive, were 'too perfect', at least according to a Prussian traveller journeying from London to Newmarket in the early nineteenth century.

Essex and Hertfordshire had the advantage of being close to London. From medieval times onwards, these two counties had provided for many of the needs of the city population. The network of rivers and the sea-coast traffic in Essex encouraged the movement of crops and livestock to the city, with the returning barges being used to bring back manure off the streets. As far as crops were concerned, wheat and barley were both important: the wheat for bread and the barley for beer (in fact, the eastern counties later became important brewing centres). The vegetables that were produced were used either as fodder for the livestock or were sold off in the markets. Versatility was certainly the watchword: dairy cattle, sheep and pigs were all much in evidence as well. As de la Rochefoucauld pointed out, the area includes 'every kind of soil, every kind of cultivation'.

This versatility was widespread: the dairy farmers of 'high Suffolk' (around Framlingham), the Norfolk poultry farmers and breeders of black cattle and the graziers of the Thames marshes (renowned for their salt-fed lamb) all benefited equally.

The excellent farming conditions of these eastern counties were, and still are, well known. As Defoe pointed out, the yeoman farmers had come to the area in Tudor times to take advantage of them. They were the first of many settlers: in the nineteenth century came the Scottish East Coast farmers, and more recently still, the Danes and Dutch.

Farm buildings
Despite the variety of farming activity (much of which needed no special buildings) there is a considerable homogeneity in the agricultural buildings across these eastern counties. Materials may have varied, but forms hardly did so at all.

In a corn-growing area such as this, it is the large-scale barn that is the most enduring monument to agricultural enterprise and constructional

Left and top right: Hales Court barn, Norfolk, built *c.* 1480 for Henry VIII's Attorney General. Of brick construction, the barn is 184ft long. Some of the 'steads' or bays were adapted at the east end for living accommodation for farm servants. The interior (left) has fine queen posts with collar beams and braces. Stabling was inserted at a later date. There are no doors to the south.

Above: Dutch influence at Sawtry, in Cambridgeshire. Lightly dusted with snow, the ubiquitous 20th-century corrugated iron roof appears at its best.

skill. From the staggering size of the timber-framed ecclesiastical barns of Essex (such as the wheat and barley barns at Cressing) to the architect-designed multi-purpose great barn of white brick on the Holkham estate in Norfolk, examples of the barn at its most spectacular abound. Besides these, there is an astonishing number of superb smaller-scale barns.

The barn, with its basic requirements of threshing floor, two storage bays and transverse paired doors, has already been described. In this region, some special features are common: a gabled porch, or midstrey, was frequently added at entrances to shelter the farm-carts. (Curiously, in some of these barns the horse's work continued inside: it was required to tread down the heaped straw which grew to such a height that the horse had to be rescued at the end of the day by sliding down a chute!)

The oldest barns across the eastern region present a unified picture – they are timber-framed and thatched. In the seventeenth century, Dutch influence brought specific architectural features such as the curving and stepped gables of many Norfolk barns and farmhouses.

At the time Marshall was looking at Norfolk, he found some remarkably fine barns and claimed, no doubt with exaggeration, that no barn had fewer than three threshing floors, some five or six. Certainly at that time many farmers had fallen victim to the new trends and tended to over-reach themselves, extending their farms 'in order that they might, agreeably with the fashion or frenzy of the day, become great farmers'.

Of the building materials used in the farmstead, the chalk areas provided flints (both cobbles and pebbles) and clunch; good clays for bricks were also plentiful. Clay lump was a distinctive local material and, in Essex, weather-boarded houses were much in evidence – a rare example of material and techniques normally used for outbuildings being transferred to the farmhouse itself. Colour-washed plaster covered the laths, or brick-nogging, set in fancy herringbone patterns, filled the panels between the timber-framing of the farmhouses and barns. However, wood was still a dominant building material throughout, disguised or not.

As Defoe pointed out, in the area between Yarmouth and Cromer (on the Norfolk/Suffolk border) virtually every building on the farm was made of wood: 'old planks, beams, wales and timbers etc, the wrecks of ships and ruins of mariners' and merchants' fortunes'. De la Rochefoucauld also commented on the use of wood:

behind the houses are the usual farm buildings – barns, a stable and so on. They are built of boards, joined together and painted brown, the whole being roofed with thatch. This type of building is very common, and, I imagine, the cheapest; it lasts a long time, the boards are generally of fir or pine and are preserved by their own resin and a coat of paint.

In the early nineteenth century brick was much in use – both the local red brick and the 'white' Suffolk type. By this period the Dutch influence in details of style was waning. Thatching was still being carried out, although with an expensive but durable local alternative to straw – reeds from the Norfolk Broads. Marshall estimated that the new thatch would last fifty years and 'with small adjustment' could be stretched a further thirty or forty.

Livestock

Cattle in this area were not provided with permanent shelter, apart from well-fenced foldyards, although they did have rubbing posts. Proper cattle byres, where they existed, tended to have rounded pillars, specifically for that purpose. The Norfolk pigs fared rather better as far as purpose-built accommodation was concerned: they had unusually high sties into which the farmer could walk upright, instead of 'creeping in', the usual practice.

The mixed foldyard seems to have been an East Anglian idea; as de la Rochefoucauld described it, all

Above: Farmhouse dating from 1595 at Elsworth, Cambridgeshire. The house is timber-framed. The central projection on this north side encloses the stair and is matched on the south side by a storeyed-over, gabled porch.

Right: A thatched barn with tiled lean-tos in the Waveney Valley. The lean-tos are later additions to provide shelter for the cattle. The midstrey (the gabled entrance) has great double doors to allow the waggons through.

Above: A timber-framed farmhouse at Metfield in Suffolk. The box-framing becomes close-studded at attic height, as this view of the gable end shows. There is a fine Tudor brick chimney stack and the house retains its original mullioned windows.

the animals came in, pigs included. Marshall found it divided up by fencing into warm and snug corners for the various beasts. The Frenchman, with an evident liking for the picturesque in farming, remarked that it was always 'pleasant to stroll through a farmyard of this kind', but added thoughtfully, 'those who are afraid of animals can walk round the edge.' In the farm in his description, the barns were in fine condition and all land under cultivation was completely surrounded by ditches – keeping the cattle in their place.

Top right: Stepped gables and diaper brickwork on a fine Tudor chimney-stack at a farmhouse at Norton Little Green, Suffolk. The weather-boarded barn at the same farm, right, is a later addition.

Victorian improvements

By the next era, that of Victorian 'high farming', the cattle were being fattened under cover in intensive conditions. Progressive landowners in East Anglia were building up model farmsteads much as their eighteenth-century forebears had done but to new specifications. Sometimes an already great estate continued to expand; for example, Coke, at Holkham, had spent an estimated £400,000 on buildings and other permanent improvements between 1776 and 1815. In the next generation over £10,000 was spent in one year alone on further estate building works.

Eastern England harboured some of the most exciting experimental farms. Essex was much developed along progressive lines, and brick-built farmsteads with patterned polychrome brickwork and flourishes, such as wrought-iron field gates and fencing, can be found all over the county. Architects had moved into the designing of the farm and one of them, Frederick Chancellor, ran up numerous schemes. In one album of designs alone he presented twenty-five proposals: his farmsteads, and others like them, incorporated an engine-house which powered the preparation of foodstuffs for livestock as well as the threshing machine or sawmill – a job which, on the noted experimental farm of J. J. Mechi, a self-made businessman turned farmer, was done by a six-horse-power engine.

However, as well as progressive activities there were still some retrograde practices. Caird found plenty of examples of the old practice whereby the tenant was forced to erect wooden buildings, from his own trees, at his own cost. This meant, quite often, that buildings in need of replacement were treated to botched-up repairs instead.

Overleaf: Model farm at Eccleston, Cheshire, one of many built on the Grosvenor Estate near Chester in the late 19th century. The group dates from 1875–80.

Below: Farmhouse (1866) and dairy (1862) at Park Farm, Wimpole, Cambridgeshire. The dairy (right) has a polygonal extension at the rear.

Right: Straw bales in Norfolk – one of the most efficiently farmed areas in the country.

Below right: The Great Barn at Holkham Hall, built c. 1790. A field barn for the storage of crops and for animal shelter, its grandeur symbolizes the aspirations of the Agricultural Revolution.

Arable landscape at Ashwell, Hertfordshire. The large farmhouse dates from the 16th and 17th centuries.

Although the landscape of eastern England is punctuated by groups of traditional buildings, they are overshadowed by the massive new sheds of modern farming on the grandest scale. The landscape is much changed. Hedges have gone from large parts of the region, field boundaries no longer break up the slightly swelling horizon with their former regularity, and pastures along the river valleys have often been eradicated in favour of arable land, long, low, battery-farming sheds or even housing estates.

Farmers on the fringes of London have had to intensify production to balance sharply increasing land values; great sweeps of glass-houses in Essex, Hertfordshire and Bedfordshire are now part of the farming landscape, together with fields of vegetables and those distinctive groups of small-holdings which mark Government intervention after World War I, when people were induced back to the land.

Above left: Farms within the village at Plungar, Vale of Belvoir.

Left: Tixover, Leicestershire – the dovecote, left, a symbol of medieval manorial rights.

The farmsteads of the eastern counties have always been in the vanguard of agricultural change, from the seventeenth century to the present. They stand as witness to successful agricultural practice sustained over a long period, sometimes recently at the expense of the landscape itself. Prairie farming, as it became known in the 1960s, was to convert parts of the eastern counties into windswept dust-bowls, with, at worst, the only feature a severe shelter belt of trees hiding the farm itself. Yet much of East Anglia and the adjoining counties has, remarkably, preserved its agricultural past despite its constant contact with the new. Inevitably, some of the fine timber-framed corn barns characteristic of much of the area have fallen into decay, yet many still retain a function and their tiled (even, occasionally, thatched) roof ridges are reassuring bulwarks rising among the ranks of featureless sheds that surround them. Juxtaposition of old and new can give new emphasis to both – the fine legacy of farm buildings that remains in the eastern counties does just that.

169

The East Midlands and Humberside

Humberside, Leicestershire, Lincolnshire, Nottinghamshire, Northamptonshire and north Buckinghamshire

The Midland counties, and the eastern Wolds which shield them from the North Sea, present a picture of agricultural efficiency and organization hard to match elsewhere in Britain – or even in Europe for that matter. Largely a flat landscape, its great valleys, of the Trent and the Ouse, scarcely make an impression. Only the Wolds, rolling seawards, break the low horizon.

At the close of the seventeenth century, Celia Fiennes looked down on the Vale of Belvoir spanning parts of Leicestershire and Lincolnshire and saw

> a prospect more than 20 mile about shewing the diversityes of Cultivations and produce of the Earth, the land is very rich and fruitfull, so the green Meadows with the fine Corn fields . . . there is all sorts of Graine besides, and Plaines and Rivers and great Woods . . .

Elsewhere in Leicestershire she noticed 'very rich country, red land'; it had much in common with the Vale of Aylesbury further south.

For centuries most of the land in this area has lent itself to a prosperous pattern of mixed agriculture, although to the east the pattern has been less smooth. Changes of emphasis between corn and livestock, livestock and corn have caused constant alteration to both landscape and buildings.

Some districts, such as the Isle of Axholme on the south bank of the Humber, and the northern

The geometric landscape of Timberland Fen, Lincolnshire.

170

fens, have pursued a separate path, in respect of both the pattern of agriculture and land ownership. In this low-lying area, with its very rich soil, the need for drainage had encouraged communal action. All the population had a stake and share in the land, and feudalism had little hold. In this part, an intensive husbandry was developed to make use of the rich land and the smaller holdings.

The eastern flank

This part of the area owes much to the advances in agricultural methods made in Norfolk in the early years of the eighteenth century. The dry Wolds of Lincolnshire and east Yorkshire, supporting a mixture of pasture and arable cornland, were ideal for the sheep and corn husbandry practised on downland all over the country. They had seen a cycle of agricultural change. Early medieval husbandry in these regions had been chiefly arable, in open fields. Then, with the late medieval explosion in wool prices, these great expanses had been given over to sheep walks and rabbit warrens. In the eighteenth century, with enclosure, they became, once again, important arable regions, and have remained so to this day.

The built landscape of farming here, formed by the mid-nineteenth century at the latest and largely still evident, is firmly divided between the village-based farms of pre-enclosure times, the occasional older isolated farm (a remnant of a lost village) and the large 'new' outlying farms with their attendant series of far-flung buildings. Some of the foldyards (known here as 'crewyards') of larger arable farms had been developed into separate farmsteads, perhaps with a house for the bailiff or chief cow-man. In the village-based farms, the buildings surrounded the farmhouse in a more or less haphazard fashion, often lining up their back walls along the village street. The later, solitary farmsteads were always constructed according to a plan – albeit sometimes rudimentary – with a formal yard and barns, shelter sheds, waggon sheds and other miscellaneous buildings gathered around the house. Water was marshalled into a pond or was obtained from a deeply excavated well or pump.

Constant agricultural change over the whole of the eastern area demanded new buildings and the adaptation of old ones. As arable agriculture pushed out livestock in the Hanoverian period, so the need was for more stabling for plough horses and better shelter for the machinery. The cattle accommodation was secondary: their function as providers of fertilizer was paramount and thus the crewyards were sited out in the fields where the manure was needed. Scattered sites across the farm eliminated time-wasting treks to and from the central farmstead. Farmers at this period were time and motion men, *avant la lettre*.

The outlying farm had another, hidden advantage in the minds of landowner and agent. From a moral standpoint, it was thought that tenants and farm labourers should not be exposed to the evils of the public house and in the new scheme of things, with everybody isolated in immense stretches of open country, there was less temptation to stray.

After the depression in farming following the Napoleonic Wars, agriculture began to improve,

172

and a new set of priorities was introduced on the farm. With the improved yield in winter crops, larger numbers of cattle were being kept, as is demonstrated in a careful list of improvements carried out on a farm near Louth on the Lincolnshire Wolds between 1829 and 1849. Among the considerable range of works carried out on both house and farm buildings there were the following: in 1830, a 'three part calf shade' is added, then, three times between 1831 and 1836, enlargements in the provision for waggons were carried out, and in the latter year the crewyards were enlarged as well. In 1838 the redundant cart-sheds (presumably built for smaller-scale equipment) were converted into piggeries. Three years later two more crewyards were constructed. Yet by the 1860s, when 'high farming' was in full swing, it would be necessary to roof over all cattle accommodation. (Imported foodstuffs were making their feeding more expensive, and dilution of manure

with rainwater and the weakening of the animals in cold and wet weather were considered wasteful.) And so all the shelters and yards run up in the preceding thirty years would be rendered redundant. As much as anywhere in the country, the Wolds bore the brunt of the swings and roundabouts of agricultural development during the later eighteenth and much of the nineteenth century. The evidence is offered in their buildings, largely of brick – both locally produced and, later, brought by canal and railway – and roofed in tiles or slates.

The central counties
Further west, in the rich Midland counties of Leicestershire, Rutland, Nottinghamshire and

Medieval barn, at Church Farm, Thorpe Waterville, Northamptonshire. The chimneyed barn with its chamfered windows may preserve traces of a fortified manor on this site from 1301. The interior (far left) shows the king post roof and the tie-beams.

much of the rest of Lincolnshire, there was strong contrast between those areas which were enclosed early by agreement and those which had fought against the takeover of the common land and the partitioning of open fields into demarcated farms.

The relics of the open-field farming pattern remain in those farmsteads of this part of the region which are ensconced in the village itself; the exceptions are the Victorian additions out in the fields. Materials here include a fine range of stones, with the dominant one, limestone, tinged orange or even a dark burnt sienna, and the brick that creeps in at the extremities of the area – in Lincolnshire, Nottinghamshire and north Buckinghamshire.

In the late eighteenth century, Marshall observed the widespread use of brick and the continued use of oak (which was too expensive elsewhere and difficult to find). He also noticed that thatch was giving way to 'knobbed plain tiles', though blue slate was preferred in Leicestershire. The build-ings, 'large, substantial and commodious', reflected the continued prosperity of an agriculture which now benefited from a canal system, as well as a great network of rivers; to this excellent transport system the railway was soon to be added.

Marshall found a number of villages still working the open-field system (only the famed Laxton now remains), but he also found a number of progressive farmers prepared to read of and to experiment in the new ways, sometimes urged on by their sons. On these more progressive farms, he noticed all sorts of small details: barn floors that were of boards fitted tongue-and-groove over brick (it deterred vermin), and brick used for two- or three-foot-high coped walls around the stackyards and for mangers in the stabling. The open foldyards presumably reflected a climate not consistently cold or wet enough to merit proper cow-byres, although in the nineteenth-century move towards intensive stock rearing the animals moved under cover, here

174

as elsewhere.

One other detail Marshall commented upon was the practice of placing rubbing posts in the pig-sties. The effect could be seen in their faces, he claimed. 'In a few days they cleared away their coats, cleaned their skins and became sleekly haired' – a contrast to their former 'broken, ragged' selves and their 'dull, heavy countenances'. Graziers used trees or special posts for cows, to serve much the same ends. For, as Marshall pointed out, it was 'not probable that any animal should thrive while afflicted with pain or uneasiness'.

Pigs were an important section of the livestock population – in Leicestershire in particular, hence the famous Melton Mowbray pies and pork meat production. Dairying in the Vale of Aylesbury in Buckinghamshire and cheese-making in Leicester-shire allowed for a prosperous small-scale pastoral agriculture. Farmhouses included the usual dairies and cheese stores typical of dairying regions.

Wealth and industrialization

Only on the western extremity of this region did the march of industrialization affect the agriculture. The effects of the rise in population and spread of urban tentacles took the same form here as else-where. Around Nottingham, Caird noted that 'the interests of the country become more immediately subservient to those of the town.'

This was also the area dominated by a handful of vast landed estates, the region known as the 'Dukeries', which spilled into Derbyshire and Yorkshire. Though some landlords followed the best traditions of enlightened management, the Midlands had more than its share of rapacious

Opposite: Stone-built farmhouse at Beachampton in Buckinghamshire, built in the early 17th century, and much adapted and altered, as is indicated by the irregular form of the cross-wings and gables.

Above: Winter view of a gabled 17th-century ironstone farm of impressive size on the village street at Preston, Leicestershire. The setting is typical of many farms in the east Midlands counties.

175

landowners, and landlord-tenant relationships were notoriously bad: 'the tenant has often three rents to pay; one in money, another in feeding the game, and a third for the support of the hedgerow timber,' wrote Caird. In 1873 Rutland had the largest percentage of landed estates to its area of any county – 53 per cent. Northumberland came next with 50 per cent.

The efficient estates throughout the Midlands and eastern counties, from the Sykes's in East Yorkshire to the Spencers' in Northamptonshire, were able to supply much of their own requirements; in some respects self-sufficiency still governed their organization. The Yarborough Estate in Lincolnshire, for example, covering 55,000 acres in the 1830s, had five brickyards. Elsewhere timber yards and sawmills produced further building materials; and a clerk of works and a labour force carried out the operation. The farmhouses and cottages that spread across these vast empires were marked out by their architectural style: a Tudor detail there, a Gothic touch here, the paintwork and the monogram above the porch made it plain whose they were.

By the mid-Victorian period, when Caird was travelling between one such great estate and the next, it was becoming obvious that, on the whole, the businessmen who had become landowners were better landlords – improving land, building widely and treating their tenants fairly. Not all hereditary landlords could present such a virtuous face; the worldliness of the industrialist stood him in better stead to take on the new directions of farming with energy and imagination.

The improvements in transport of the Victorian age brought uniformity in materials, and the Midlands in large part bear the impression of that standardization. The replacement of the tomato-red pantiles of the eastern area with factory-made tiles, and of the spongey-looking plum bricks across the northern stretch of these counties with harsh, shiny red bricks of uniform size, standard bonding, and razor-sharp pointing brought considerable change in detail to the buildings of the farmstead.

The Midland counties express clearly through the form and arrangement, siting and plan of their farm buildings the way in which farming had evolved in the different areas. The cottages surrounding the manor house in many Leicestershire villages, or the farms pressed up to the village street in southern Lincolnshire, or Northamptonshire, show respectively the longevity of the manorial system and the remnants of the open-field agriculture of which W. G. Hoskins observes 'agreed and common action . . . was a good foundation for any civilisation.' Then out on the arable eastern stretches the isolated farms, rarely built before the latter decades of the eighteenth century, tell of agricultural innovation. If the new methods of cultivation did not come as soon here as to Norfolk, the buildings certainly did. The Sykes's model farms around Sledmere predated the works carried out by Coke in north Norfolk by some years.

All these clues remain in the landscape, though to the south of the area the scale of farming and the emphasis on cash crops grown on a vast scale have obscured the nature of farming in the past. Sometimes the landscape has lost its subtlety in the process; there are areas which have no focal point – no trees, no field boundaries, no buildings. Yet that scale, and that pattern of agriculture, when translated to the Wolds, has produced some of the most dramatic and unpopulated countryside in Britain, with rolling acres of cornland, hidden dry valleys and, here and there, a stately farmhouse just below a rise. Undiscovered by tourism, and with its attractions closely dependent on the seasons and the patterns of light, it is one area of England in which a largely treeless and hedge-free agricultural landscape has an unexpected and unusual beauty.

Harvesting vegetables in the rich loamy soils around the Wash, at Holland Fen in Lincolnshire. This is some of the best agricultural land to be found in the country, most of it reclaimed from swamp land and from the sea in the great drainage programmes of the 19th century.

Top: Cart shelter on an 18th-century model farm on the Wolds at Sledmere, North Humberside.

Above: Pig troughs set into the wall of a 19th-century farmyard at Kirkby Green, Lincolnshire.

Right: Arcaded brick cart-shed with granary overhead at Swallow Grange, Lincolnshire. Typical of the well-built new farms of the early 19th century.

Below: Bringing in the newly shorn fleeces at a farm in Abthorpe, Northamptonshire and right, the usual paraphernalia of farming at the same farm.

Left: A corrugated iron Dutch barn, sited out among the fields of Aynhoe, Northamptonshire – the 20th-century replacement for the thatched rick.

Below: Farm near Brill, Buckinghamshire, sited on the crest of a hill. The vast chimney stack is an indication of a largely Tudor house.

The West Midlands and Welsh Borders

Hereford and Worcester, Shropshire, central Staffordshire, Cheshire, lowland Lancashire, Warwickshire

There are two dominant types of agricultural landscape within this region: the small-scale, wooded country with its tidy, smooth hills bordering Wales, and the flat, rich countryside dissected by the great lazy ribbons of the Severn and Avon as they make their way towards their joint estuary. Despite differences in topography and obvious variations in farming, this is, as a western region, a countryside of more grass than grain, in which buildings of timber or brick predominate.

Much of Hereford and Worcester and part of Shropshire are hilly areas; the Malvern hills, the foothills of the various Welsh mountain ranges and Wenlock Edge are the outstanding features. Rolling around them is an undulating landscape which until the sixteenth century was largely wooded. The topography encouraged small-scale intensive agriculture; the abundant timber dictated the building materials and encouraged a tradition of fine craftsmanship. The evidence of the high quality carpentry of the timber-framed houses and barns points to a prosperous farming population of owner-occupiers. The counties of Hereford and Worcester, like the Weald of Kent and Sussex which they resemble in many ways, became famous for their fruit and hops.

The lowlands in the southern and western areas were gradually cleared of woodland from the Tudor period onwards, and to the north they remained

Border landscape near Clun, Shropshire.

largely uncultivated until the nineteenth century because of water-logged soils and impassable marshes (the infamous 'mosses'). As such, they were to support a very different system of agriculture and to attract a different kind of farmer: the large landowner or the small dairy farmer. The former invested his capital in improvements, the latter was able to supply the growing urban areas resulting from industrial enterprise. The Industrial Revolution, in fact, began in the Severn Gorge in the early eighteenth century, and these mid-western counties experienced the pressures of industry and its workforce long before other parts of the country, including the Potteries, or the north west of this region.

Fruit and hop growing

As in the Weald, the dominant crops of fruit and hops give a characteristically abundant look to the landscape of Hereford and Worcester. Celia Fiennes, standing on the Malvern Hills (or English Alps as she melodramatically called them) observed the scene 300 years ago:

> on the other side is Herrifordshire which appears like a Country off Gardens and Orchards, the whole Country being very full of fruite trees etc, it lookes like nothing else, the apple pear trees etc are so thick even in their corn fields and hedgerows.

The prosperous Vale of Evesham, to the other side of the Malvern Hills, would have given her much the same impression.

Apples and pears, then as now, were grown both for eating and for making cider and perry, a process which, like the drying of hops, required its own purpose-built structures. Even small cottages seem to have had a separate bay given over to cider-making and, in a reasonable-sized farm, there would be two cider-mills, one for the men and one for the farmer and his family. Marshall observed here that 'a mill house on an orchard farm is as necessary as a barn'. The design was similar to those used in the West Country.

The hop (a quarter of the crop of England and Wales in the early nineteenth century was grown in Herefordshire) introduced the need for kilns, although some hop drying was done by merely turning the crop in a well-aired space. The early drying rooms and kilns were incorporated into existing buildings, sometimes well-disguised since they were taxable. Often the only clue to such a room is the ventilation, perhaps a simple device such as a ridge-tile laid crossways on the bridge of the roof. It was not until the 1830s that the distinctive form of the circular, and later the square, hop kiln entered the landscape in this part of the country, although hops had been grown since at least the early seventeenth century.

Since hops required space for only two months of the year, September and October, during which the harvesting and drying took place, one answer was to use a dual-purpose structure. For this a sizable granary was developed, which took the form of a service wing of the farmhouse with the other activities (dairy, laundry or pantry, for example) below. The interesting feature of this arrangement was that it was disguised by the trappings of domestic architecture so that at first glance it appears to be properly part of the house, in fenestration, materials and detail. If the hops were processed in this part of the house, a clue remains with the treading holes, under which hung the pockets (the long canvas bags in which the hops were stored) and into which the labourer would climb in order to further compress the hops. He presumably rose to floor height as the bag filled.

Mixed agriculture in the border counties

Besides fruit and hops, Hereford, Worcester and Shropshire supported a prosperous mixed agricultural pattern. Evidence of this agriculture comes from Buttas Manor, in Herefordshire, where it was recorded in 1623 that a large new frame of buildings had been put up. It included six lofts for malting and other purposes, 'fairstable with chambers over, two glazed and ceiled', two barns (one new and tiled), a large 'beast-house', large 'sheepcot', swine-house, pigeon-house, and a hop yard with 6,000 poles. The conditions encouraged the consolidation of relatively large holdings and the poor were pushed into the forests and wasteland to form squatter settlements where they could. The random pattern of scattered settlements can be seen in the Forest of

Dean today – an area where the poor found a living by combining small-holding with iron smelting, for example.

For the prosperous late sixteenth- and early seventeenth-century farmer there were abundant materials with which to build, including timber for the cruck-framed barns and for the farmhouse, which by this period was being constructed in the more modern post and truss system. There was also a pink-grey sandstone and brick. The reds and pinks, highlighted by the exuberant black and white half-timbered buildings (including some in which the timbering was faked, painted onto the white-washed plaster or brick) combine to give this part of the countryside a sparkling, colourful look to this day. As in the neighbouring Welsh counties, small farmers in this area held tenaciously to the longhouse tradition long after it had died out else-where. For the remarkably unchanging life of the small farmer in the border counties we have the record of Kilvert's diary. He tells of the oxen still in use, of dairying in the farmhouse and he sketches in much of late nineteenth-century agricultural life in that quiet backwater. Only the threshing machines, often driven by water power in this area of hill streams and torrents and never-failing rainfall, had introduced change.

Large-scale farming – Staffordshire

In Staffordshire, the already strong contrasts in landscape and farming became more marked in the late eighteenth century, when the uplands to the north (the Potteries) and to the south (Wolver-hampton and Dudley) became heavily industrial-ized. Only the central band was left to agriculture and this was owned by a posse of large landowners, many of them agricultural reformers – Lord Anson at Shugborough, Josiah Wedgwood (son of the great potter), the Marquess of Stafford and Lord Bradford among them. As was noted in a Board of Agriculture report for the county, 'the demesnes of these gentlemen may be looked upon as a sort of school.' Between them, these landowners trans-formed the landscape with their drainage schemes, their neat hawthorn hedges and their meadows, artificially flooded to improve the fertility – so-called 'floating meadows'.

After that came the buildings: in the latter half of the eighteenth century, model farms representing the most advanced thinking in the early decades of improvement, and triumphs of engineering and practicality in early Victorian times. By the time of Caird's visit, enterprising tenants were establishing enormous fields (100 acres each on one farm); one had devised a system of condensing milk, and on one of the Duke of Sutherland's farms the farm buildings included a water-powered threshing ma-chine, livestock feeding-houses, root houses and steaming houses (where the foodstuffs were cooked). The wealth of the proprietors, allied to the size of their estates, meant that if anything novel was likely to be tried out, it would be here.

In the south east of the same county and in neighbouring Warwickshire much of the land was similarly in the hands of a few rich landowners. As in the Midland counties further east, there had been a long history of such ownership, leaving behind it the signs of lost medieval villages and the drainage patterns of early arable fields. The farms of post-Parliamentary enclosure date stood out in the fields, the earlier ones were within the village. Farming was mixed, but much of the land was in use for pasture. Here the brick tradition of some of the counties to the north met the timber-framing traditions of the west. In parts of Warwickshire fine oaks still stand in the hedges to remind us of the great Forest of Arden that covered the west of the county.

Land improvement versus industrialization

To the north, in the important dairying counties of Cheshire and south Lancashire (the latter also famed for its fattening of store cattle which had come from Wales, eating the farmers' crops along the way), the land area was being constantly in-creased. The treacherous mosses which had so im-peded the construction of the railway line between Manchester and Liverpool, and the low-lying water-logged ground of much of the area required con-certed action. In the mid-nineteenth century the Marquess of Westminster, according to Caird, was providing his tenants with a million drainage tiles a year, and bearing a third of the labour costs of laying them.

Cattle sheds now inhabited by sheep at Stoke St. Milborough, Shropshire. Fodder would be stored above and pushed down to the animals. Sheep are generally considered hardy enough to survive without a shelter, except at lambing time.

All over this area, itinerant Irish labourers were useful additional hands for such jobs; the proximity to industrial centres, as elsewhere in the North West, had its pros and cons – it was both an incentive to the small dairy farmer and it presented the problems of trespass, loss of land and of difficulty

in keeping a stable labour force at wages lower than could be gained in industry. Describing the outskirts of Manchester on the first page of *Mary Barton*, Mrs Gaskell makes a comparison between the old black-and-white farmhouse, amidst its setting of garden and pasture, and the neighbouring manufacturing centre. The area was then, and still is, dotted with half-timbered houses and timber-framed barns as reminders of the pre-Industrial age. Mrs Gaskell's was an accurate picture of the way in which the reminders of the rural past interrupted the march of urbanization.

Similarly, the Potteries had faced the problems brought about by the growth of industry and its consequent inroads into farming land. The farmers were either driven away or were left as desultory part-time small-holders. However, in some areas, as in Ironbridge, industrialization had its benefits: there, farms were developed specifically to cater for the new work force – built on land owned by the iron master or industrialists. The rapid wealth created by the new-found industrial prosperity created a new breed of landowner who bought up large tracts of land in the further corners of these counties.

In this area of the North West the brick buildings of the eighteenth and nineteenth century predominate (tax had come off bricks in 1784) – some bricks were of the small locally fired variety and others the later, harder, factory types, such as the Staffordshire blues.

These central-western English counties demonstrate two extremes: some of the earliest commercially successful farming areas in the country and some of the formerly most intransigent pieces of ground to be found in Britain, wrested back from bog and moss by enormous effort in the nineteenth century. The contrast between the fabric of the respective buildings is telling. The gnarled timber frames and small crumbly bricks from which the farmsteads of the early ventures were constructed differ sharply from the neat, standardized sets of buildings which mark the path of those later efforts. As elsewhere, the buildings of the farm clearly indicate the requirements of the agriculture that had shaped them, and the resources that were to hand.

Right: The dovecote
(foreground) and farmhouse at
Dormston in Hereford and
Worcester. The buildings,
spectacular examples of
box-framing, were built in
1663. The tiled 'weatherings' on
the dovecote and house deflect
rain off the walls.

Far right: Timber-framed
farmhouse, dated 1647, at
Weston, Cheshire. It is a good
example of the solid geometrical
carpentry of the region; grander
houses tended to have more
decorative flourishes.

Right: These 14th-century
cruck roof timbers of a
farmhouse at Longtown,
Herefordshire, are an early and
important survival of a type of
construction associated
particularly with the Welsh
Marches. The post-and-truss
system was, however, adopted
for important buildings in the
16th and 17th centuries. Note
the pegs, locking the timbers
together.

Far right: Architect-designed
farmyard on the Duke of
Westminster's Grosvenor Estate
near Chester. The 19th-century
building has a touch of half-
timbering to echo the regional
traditions.

Far left: Elaborate Gothic glazing and decorative ventilation holes on a brick granary at Kinnerton, Cheshire. Sadly, the left-hand window details have disappeared.

Left: A 19th-century brick-built Dutch barn at Thornton-le-Moors, Cheshire, flanked by more recent barns. The wide barn, right, is a recent addition – no building before the late 19th century could have spanned such a width.

Left: Brick farm buildings at Alvanley Hall, Cheshire. The projecting barn door, large enough for waggons to enter, is known as a midstrey. The upper storey is marked on the outside by the string course, and ventilation slits echo those used on medieval barns.

Above: Local red sandstone and brick has been used for the farmhouse and buildings at Ness in the Wirral. As recommended by the agricultural theorists, the farmhouse has turned its back on the farmyard. The building to the left, provided stabling for working horses, with the fodder stored overhead.

Top: Agricultural landscape near Alvanley, Cheshire.

Left: Modern field barns at Stoke St. Milborough, Shropshire.

Right: Shropshire landscape in the Clee Hills. Trees along the stream represent earlier boundaries than the neat hedges beyond, denoting Parliamentary enclosure.

Below: A mighty farmhouse at Hopton Cangeford, Shropshire. For a clue to its size, see the range of chimneys rearing behind. To the right, a 19th-century cattle yard; to the left, traditional livestock sheds.

The Pennines and North-eastern Uplands

Yorkshire, Derbyshire and the Staffordshire and Lancashire Pennines

The character of this tract of landscape is rugged and rolling by turns, dour and windswept, lush and damp according to altitude, with many similarities with the region immediately to its north. High rainfall, little sunshine and soils veering between the light poor ground of the hills and the heavy grasslands of the valleys make farming in this part of the world a tough business. It is largely pastoral, much of it in remote hill farms, many of which have to contend with badly drained ground supporting little more than reeds, bracken and rough heather. The Pennines cut through this area from north to south, broken into by the Yorkshire Dales and a succession of smaller valleys. To the east lie the Cleveland Hills and the North Yorkshire Moors. South Derbyshire, the Vale of York, and the areas to the south and west constitute the only extensive lowland landscape. Stone is the predominant building material and provides, with the bracken-covered hills, a muted palette of grey, green and gold. Only in the eastern areas do the russet pantiles warm the picture.

The effects of industry

On closer inspection it can be seen that much of the farming pattern in this region has been affected both directly and indirectly by the disruptive nature of industry. Some areas close to the major manufacturing centres have been able to benefit by

Field barns, near Muker, Swaledale.

intensive cultivation, or dairying, and even further distant areas found themselves depending more and more on the urban markets for the sale of their produce. As Defoe observed, the areas around Halifax (and other Yorkshire textile centres, such as Leeds, Huddersfield, Bradford and Wakefield) 'must necessarily have their provisions from other parts of the country. This, then, is a subsistence to the other parts of the country . . .'

The Industrial Revolution, which after all had hardly begun at the time of Defoe's visit, not only brought increased demands on the agricultural hinterland, but perhaps more significantly, new farmers who provided stiff competition for the less forward-thinking existing farmers.

In the West Riding of Yorkshire, where wool was the main industry, clothiers combined weaving and dairying on small-holdings of about twenty acres. Successful tradesmen and rich businessmen were already, in Defoe's day, 'taking the position of the old gentry of the country'. This process, whereby within a generation or two industrial wealth shifted to the land, has continued ever since. Many of the improving landlords of the late eighteenth century had come to their estates by this route.

In the Lancashire Pennines, an area of harsh moorland, the growth of the factory-based cotton industry in the nineteenth century did not co-exist happily with the small hill farmer. The industry, being factory-based rather than relying on out-workers like the woollen industry of Yorkshire, tended to absorb the space for housing, pushing out the farmer or, if he remained, ensuring that he had a difficult time alongside the new urban sprawl. Only the unenterprising and sluggish remained. Though 'possessing an insatiable market at their doors for everything a farm produces, the very flowers in the farmer's garden being convertible into money' as Caird pointed out, the Pennine farmers missed or wasted oppor-

Range of buildings on a mixed farm at Adel, near Leeds, all built of the local stone and tiled with slates. The buildings represent a mixture of storage and livestock shelter: the arches at low level by the gate to the farmhouse are pig-troughs. The farm has probably been added to over a considerable period – the opposite of the planned farmyard of the late 18th- and 19th-century theorists.

tunities. In any event, railway links had, by this period, reinforced the habit of importing goods from elsewhere; as Defoe had already described, 'their corn comes up in great quantities out of Lincoln, Nottingham and the East Riding, their black cattle and horses from the North Riding, their cheese out of Cheshire and Warwickshire.' He also mentioned cattle from lowland Lancashire. In the intervening century or more, not much has changed, except the volume of demand and the sources of supply.

West Yorkshire and the Pennines

With the large holdings of ecclesiastical estates, and with good quality timber and plenty of stone, West Yorkshire has a fine legacy of barns – including some impressive tithe barns. The aisled barn, common to Lancashire and West Yorkshire, seems to have been adapted as a dual-purpose structure with the cattle tethered down the side aisles. The barn at East Riddlesden Hall, owned by the National Trust, has eight bays, with great oak supports mounted on stone bases, and was equipped with special entrances for the clearance of manure, on the pattern of the standard shippon.

Another building type common to this area, and shared with the Lake District, is the laithe-house. This was the late eighteenth-century, early nineteenth-century development of house and farm buildings (byre and barn) under one roof. Unlike the ancient longhouse plan, the two parts are quite self-contained and the laithe-house was built at one time, rather than representing a series of accretions. As it was most popular in the central Pennines, it was presumably the farmstead preferred by the man who combined farming with work in the cloth industry.

Yorkshire Dales

Although it appears that in the early medieval period the Yorkshire Dales had been partly in arable cultivation (the terraced land remains as evidence), dairying came to replace corn-growing. In the late medieval period, cheese-making was based on ewes' milk, rather than cows', but the latter usurped the sheep from this function as their yields improved. Because of the emphasis on small-scale dairy farming, most of the important farming functions took place in the house itself. It included a beef loft, in which pickled carcases and hams could hang over the winter, and a dairy and cooling room for the cheese. Pigs were often housed nearby since they could use the waste products from dairying and they helped to provide enough meat to see the family through the winter. Self-sufficiency was essential in these remote places, cut off by weather and lack of means of access for long periods in the winter.

Milking was done in the fields in summer and the milk brought down to the farm by pony. In winter, the milking was carried out in the dark cattle sheds. The pony, also used to bring hay down from higher pastures, had adequate quarters, and sometimes the stable included a small room overhead for the farmhand, if the farm merited such help. Other buildings of the farmstead were a flagged cart-shed and, perhaps, a 'hogg-house' for young sheep. The cart-shed might, like the barns in the arable areas, be used as a village hall, for entertainment.

Of all the buildings of the farm, it is the field barn, built for the storage of hay over winter, that is a particular feature of these upland landscapes and especially that of the Dales. Parts of the Dales had been enclosed by the beginning of the seventeenth century and the sturdy dry-stone walls that formed the field boundaries made a dense mesh across the valley bottoms and up the hillsides, punctuated by box-like two-storey barns, in which were stored hay supplies and animal shelters, if necessary. Emphasized by the optical effects of distance, these barns and walls give the Dales an oddly built-up appearance. With derelict barns and tumble-down walls, some stretches look like abandoned towns.

In the Peak District of Derbyshire, where the bleached limestone and blond grasslands make a

Wharfedale farmhouse, above, and Bishopdale farmhouse, right, both with barn and cattle byre attached on the longhouse pattern. The buildings to the left of the Wharfedale farmouse represent later additions to the farm-buildings as more extensive space became necessary for storage of larger scale equipment and fodder.

198

sharp contrast to the millstone grit of the Pennines, the landscape is also marked out by walls and sporadic barns. Celia Fiennes commented that near Buxton 'you scarce see a tree and no hedges all over the Country, only dry stone walls that incloses ground no other fence.' She would see little change today. In all other respects the small Pennine farms of both Derbyshire and Staffordshire share the characteristics of the Pennine farms of Lancashire and Yorkshire already described.

North-east Yorkshire

With the moorland pressing down upon the enclosed pasture, the north-east Yorkshire Dales, such as Bransdale, Farndale and Rosedale, are generally less fertile than their damp Pennine counterparts. The farms are strung along the valleys at intervals, their sites determined by the presence of a spring or beck. Often they have been planned as four-sided farmyards with the various buildings clustered round the midden, its paved causeway leading between barn and cattle shed (which perhaps share the same roof). Sometimes the longhouse pattern has been preferred, with the farmhouse on the upper contours and the attached buildings following the gradient down. Many of the later detached, symmetrical houses have

Unusually elegant farmhouses in in an area where small pastoral farms predominate. The farmhouse, above, at Thorpe near Burnsall, Wharfedale, and the farmhouse, right, at Arkingarthdale in the Yorkshire Dales, both have pedimented doorways and dressed stone quoins.

Overleaf: Farndale in the North Yorkshire moors. The houses and buildings are of stone, with pantiled roofs.

200

single-bay additions. This provided space for a farming son, or conversely for an elderly parent possibly no longer actively involved in the farm.

These small farms usually had, and tend to have still, mixed livestock. Pigs live in the outshuts of barn or cow-house, with their stone feeding-troughs punched in the outer wall nearest the farmhouse (for the farmer's wife's convenience). Poultry and geese, sheepdog and sheep, cattle and, in the past, a horse make up the full complement. Even the smallest details of the buildings are determined by their function. The sheepdog lives in a shelter hollowed out under the outside steps to the granary. The barn has a little stand by the door for a lantern, sheltered against a windy night. Outside the farmstead, water is marshalled down from its source via stone gullies and troughs; dry-stone walls have passageways through which the dog can inveigle the sheep, and which are then blocked by a single slab of stone.

Surprisingly, the original single-storey farmhouses here were timber-framed and thatched, often with ling. Rare examples of the thatching have survived but stone and pantiles are the building materials down the east of the area from the tip of north Yorkshire into the Vale of Pickering and on into Humberside. The moors themselves provided a wide range of useful materials: peat, stone, bracken, ling, mosses – all had their uses and were available as common rights.

In the lowland parts of north-eastern Yorkshire, Marshall noticed both pantiles and blue slate creeping in to replace straw and rough slates. Bricks were used in the Vale of Pickering, a dark ruby-coloured firing, which left the tomato-coloured pantiles as a pale contrast. For woodwork, oak had been superseded by the eighteenth century by deal, which was cheaper.

Above left: An 18th-century farmhouse with elegant Venetian windows at Chelmorton, Derbyshire.

Left: Pennine stone farmbuildings at Earl Stanfield, Derbyshire.

Above: Small farm on the longhouse pattern at Egton, Eskdale, north Yorkshire. The small extension to the right of the house may have been for a farm servant or relative, working as an extra hand.

Left: The 17th-century farmhouse, Woodseats Hall, near Barlow in Derbyshire. The cruck barn on page 39 belongs to the same farm.

Below left: Decorative flourishes like the finials on the gateposts and the quoins on the farm buildings add dignity to the same farm.

Above: The cow byre, or shippon as it is known locally; there is only one passageway for feeding, milking, and collecting manure.

Below: The farmyard at the same farm. The steps lead to the granary conveniently sited over the stables.

Left: Arcaded former cart-shed at a farm on the outskirts of Guisborough in Cleveland.

Below: Local stone and pantiles used for the farmbuildings at the same farm. Pantiles have the advantage of good ventilation while remaining completely watertight.

Lowland areas and modernization

The fertile and flat areas that lay south of the industrial valleys and surrounding hills were an area of advanced farming in the latter half of the eighteenth century. The large landowners at estates such as Harewood, Nostell and Wentworth Woodhouse were setting the pace. They employed architects (Daniel Lascelles was presented with an elaborate sham-gothic farmhouse design by Carr of York as early as 1760); their farming operations were highly efficient and, to reflect this, farm buildings were rebuilt and extended.

Mechanization arrived here at an early date. The rich cornlands followed the example of eastern Scotland (like Northumberland), and one of the earliest horse-wheels in the country was installed in 1790 at Nunnington, near Malton, in the Vale of Pickering. From there wheel-sheds spread into most farms, including some in hilly areas, during the next fifty years. The Board of Agriculture survey of North Yorkshire, published in 1800, seems to have been exaggerating the position somewhat in remarking that horse-wheels had 'come into general employment . . . thus the even steady and poetical sound of the thresher's flail is rarely heard resounding in the boarded barn'. To the west of the area, the wheel-house was soon a commonplace appendage to the barn, as it became in the Lake District. However, once portable threshing machines became common, they were adopted with alacrity. As a cooperative effort, it suited the small farmer well. It was for the grand farms to the south and south-west of the area to adopt the steam engines, conveyor belts and railway tracks of 'high farming'.

Derbyshire

With the nineteenth-century move to intensive breeding and fattening, as in the large pastoral farms of Derbyshire, in which the scale of livestock herds put the area on a par with Leicestershire or Durham, it was not surprising to find an innovatory arrangement for the sheep on one of the Duke of Devonshire's farms at Bakewell. Purpose-built structures for sheep were unusual. However, here in Derbyshire, sited a little way from the main farmstead and accessible to the various pastures,

was 'a nicely contrived establishment for the winter feeding of sheep'. It consisted of a central turnip-house, with a loft above (for hay, oil-cake or corn) and accommodation for a shepherd during lambing. Two uncovered yards surrounded by sheds provided protection for the sheep, and hay racks and a manger for roots ran round the entire circumference. Housed like this, sheep had improved fleece and carcases, and there were fewer casualties. The arrangement was also economical on food. Most farmers, however, thought sheep could manage without such elaborate provision, for few such edifices were built on sheep farms.

The picture today

Modern agricultural practice still finds the lowland areas divided between large, ultra-modern farming estates – continuing the progressive practices of the eighteenth and nineteenth centuries along the new lines of the late twentieth century. New buildings dot the landscape.

Although in the upland areas farmers have subsidies from various sources, the pressures of farming under hard conditions have caused many of the most exposed hill farms to be vacated, and there has been considerable amalgamation. The higher pastures are often used by a farmer in the valley for summer grazing; in winter they often remain devoid of any life at all. These are strictly family farms and the smallest units give marginal returns; many of the houses have been sold off as holiday homes, with farming just an historic association.

The problems of maintaining the tough stone farms, with their scattered field barns, are the same as in other such areas protected for their fine scenery – the Lake District, Wales and parts of the West Country. Some disused barns have become overnight stops for hill walkers, preserving their outward appearance in the landscape; others, in less remote areas, may become small workshops. Those that remain in use need to be maintained; regularly attended to, they are sturdy opponents of punishing weather and age. Left to fall apart, they soon become cairns in the landscape.

Semi-derelict buildings at Angram in Swaledale, Yorkshire; a common scene in an area where many of the outlying farmhouses and buildings are redundant.

The Northern Borders

Cumbria, Durham, Northumberland and upland Lancashire

The considerable expanse of hilly, even mountainous, ground in these counties is dominated by the small-scale upland sheep farm, and the general impression of this whole region is one of tiny hill farms, with hardy livestock running on the moors and mountainsides. The farmer of these small hill farms has a long tradition of independence dating back from yeoman owner-occupiers of the past, known in these areas as 'statesmen'. However, strong contrasts exist in the rich valleys – even in the Lake District itself, which Wordsworth described as the 'Perfect Republic of Shepherds and Agriculturists' – and on the coastal lowlands. On the larger valley and lowland farms there has been considerable change from a largely corn-based husbandry (during the seventeenth and eighteenth centuries) to an emphasis on intensive cattle rearing in the mid-nineteenth century, and then back to a more balanced and mixed agriculture in recent times.

Special characteristics of the region

Historically, the area has been dogged by two problems. The first of these was the vulnerability of the border districts to the marauding Scots (until the Union with Scotland in 1603) and the resulting well-deserved reputation for lawlessness. The built evidence of the defensive state in which the

Rough landscape with glacial morrain at Fell Foot, Little Langdale, Cumbria. The 16th- to 17th-century farm is built of local slate and stone.

212

farmers lived, especially in the border country, is the pele towers and bastles, which combined semi-fortified upper-level living accommodation with storage below. They overlooked walled courtyards in which flocks or herds could be corralled in case of danger. The only laws which were respected were those laid down by a feudal system independent of any made in southern England. After the Union, however, a modicum of stability came to the area.

The other main problem was one of remoteness from the major markets and other agricultural influence. Distance meant that little news of new ventures elsewhere filtered northward and, even in the eighteenth century, it was a largely backward agricultural zone, preserving outdated farming practices and carrying them out in anachronistic buildings.

The independent character of the area could be seen clearly in Newcastle, which, like London, preserved its own sphere of influence. Innkeepers and butchers from the city were among the most conscientious tenant farmers in Durham in the mid-nineteenth century; there were also many other part-time farmers there dividing their energies between mining and agriculture.

Geography dictated limitations over the whole area where crops were concerned. Celia Fiennes noticed

> in these Northern Countyes they have only the summer graine as barley oates pease beans and lentils noe wheate or rhye, for they are so cold and late in their years they cannot venture at the sort of tillage so have none but what they are supply'd out of other countys adjacent.

Oat bread, in fact, was the staple diet in these parts.

Even now the one enduring constraint still remains the climate. Improved strains of seed, however, are able to grow and ripen where the feebler strains had failed. (In the past, farmers in some areas used a kiln to dry out the grain.) Celia Fiennes found things remarkably verdant around Windermere; she noticed 'a great deal of good grass and summer corn and pastures in its rich land in the bottoms'.

Upland farming

Upland areas in the whole region were devoted then, as now, to sheep and there was a flourishing local cloth industry based on the market towns. Upland grazing, until the eighteenth century, was entirely unenclosed, with common rights supplied as 'stints' (allotted areas) and much is unenclosed still. The dry-stone walls and field barns attest to a new ordering of the land at a relatively late date – around the turn of the nineteenth century.

On the east side of the region, on the moorlands of Northumberland, the remnants of an intensive network of small cottages known as 'shielings' are proof of the practice of transhumance – the wholesale removal of the livestock and the farming community to higher pasture in the summer months. The practice was discontinued in this area by the seventeenth century, as the stability brought about by the Union with Scotland in 1603 meant that vigilance over herds could be relaxed somewhat. Most farmers chose to settle in the valleys but sometimes the shielings were incorporated into later farmsteads. While it existed, transhumance had an obvious influence on agricultural buildings. Because two sets of buildings were required, neither was much developed. In the sixteenth century, William Camden in his survey of the British Isles, *Britannia*, referred to the 'little cottages here and there which they call sheales and shealings'; often they were grouped in temporary hamlets, and were accompanied by stack stands, on which a supply of hay was built up.

The upland farmhouse

The traditional small farmhouse of the upland areas was generally built with house and cow-stalls under one roof, either in the form of a longhouse, cut in half by a cross-passage, or in the eighteenth century as a laithe-house, where the units were self-contained but contiguous. Both types derived benefit from the slope of the land, using as far as possible drainage systems dependent on gravity.

Right: Rear view of Kentmere Hall, Cumbria. The pele tower is 14th century, and was part-defensive, part-domestic. The 15th-century cross-wing of the house is now used as a bank barn.

Above: The charm of Kentmere Hall's stone-walled farmyard evokes the illustrations – drawn from life – of Beatrix Potter. A keen breeder of Herdwick sheep, she farmed nearby herself.

Right: Glencoyne farmhouse and range of buildings at Patterdale, near Ullswater. The building on the far right is modern, constructed with traditional materials. High-quality extensions such as these are grant-aided, but in areas of outstanding natural beauty it has been suggested that the entire extra cost of such building should be borne publically.

Below: Longhouse with bank barn in the Kentmere Valley, Cumbria. It has a 1703 datestone. The pentice roof gives protection from the elements.

Left: Spinning gallery of a barn in Coniston, Cumbria – the original purpose of the gallery was possibly for drying fleeces.

Below: Town End barn – a grand example of a bank barn, with wings and canopied gallery, at Troutbeck, Cumbria. The mullioned windows may have been taken from a house – the date, 1666, is inscribed over one of them.

As enclosure altered the landscape, the farm, still in this linked form, appeared in the village street. Few Cumbrian villages are without a number of small farmsteads lined up along the main street, their cart-sized gateways punctuating the rough stonework of the barns.

The typical upland farm unit needed little more than space for a few cattle, storage for a small quantity of grain (which might be provided within the house itself) and stabling for a hardy hill pony. Depending on the space available on site and the farm acreage this might extend into more stabling with lofts above, and even a cart-shed. Further buildings were often separated from the house, facing it across a yard, or were linked with it at right angles. The stone and slates were quarried locally and whitewash was applied to the house, to differentiate it from the utilitarian farm buildings – the opposite, oddly enough, of the practice in some parts of Wales, where buildings are whitewashed, for hygiene, and the house is left to show off its stonework undisguised.

Right: As the chimney suggests, this 19th-century farm at Alnwick, Northumberland, was steam powered on a large scale – the expertise borrowed from the local mines.

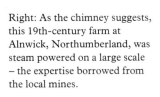

Left: View from Dyke Head Farm over open and recently formed agricultural landscape; the field patterns are probably mid-19th century, contemporary with the farm.

Above: Lower Trewhitt, Rothbury in Northumberland – a large and particularly advanced late 19th-century farm built for Lord Armstrong of Cragside. The cottages provided for farm workers are, typically, within the farmyard. The power for the mechanized farm was hydraulic.

The barns

One very localized adaptation of a farm building was the bank barn, found only in the west and south west of Lakeland. It incorporated an upper-level threshing barn with animal space and perhaps a bay for hay (the sink mow) on a lower level. Carts brought in the corn on a ramp while the animals entered directly from the farmyard. It usually lay along the contour; less commonly, across it.

Field barns, as in the southern Pennines, also operated on two levels (again to benefit from the slope of the land) but here the upper storey was purely for the storage of hay or straw, the lower for animals. Entry was from opposite sides. In Northumberland, a specific type of lowland field barn was the hemmel, a single-storey shelter shed with arched openings. Sometimes it was shared between two holdings with the boundary wall of the field corresponding with the cross wall inside the barn.

In valleys, or towards the coast, barns grew larger, reflecting the bigger grain crop. More arable land meant more oxen or horses and thus larger buildings for stabling. Cattle were milked under cover. Loose boxes were provided for calves, and adult animals were tied in pairs. Cow houses were miserable and ill-lit, with low ceilings, reflecting ignorance about the needs of livestock. Warmth was thought desirable above all else – even that obtained from steaming dung was considered helpful. The beneficial effects of cleanliness and light were not understood until Victorian times. There was limited accommodation for sheep; weaker animals could be sheltered in the 'hogg-house'.

Agricultural improvements

In lowland areas of the North East, special accommodation for fattening beef cattle was developed, as the emphasis on arable land shifted towards livestock in the mid-nineteenth century. The Durham shorthorn (first bred in the 1780s) was a phenomenally successful breed. First used for beef, it became a profitable dairy animal but in the meantime it made both County Durham and the coastal region of Northumberland among the most important livestock areas in the country.

The need for improvement or new buildings was so great that the farmer was advised to look out for some kind of economical, even temporary accommodation 'for the expenditure recommended by most of our book authorities would swamp a landlord altogether'. Caird thought wooden feeding stalls might do, using available timber and at a cost of 10s a head.

The great Northumberland estate owners were progressive agriculturally, if less often socially, and shared ideas of innovation with their counterparts down the east coast, both on the Yorkshire Wolds and in Norfolk. Various Dukes of Northumberland commissioned local architects to build farmhouses and farmsteads; Lord Armstrong, at the end of the nineteenth century, brought to farming the same spirit as he did to engineering and manufacturing: Cragside, his country house designed by Norman Shaw, was the first house to be lit by electricity. His home farm, at Lower Trewhitt, housed an elaborate sequence of hydraulic power systems, railway track, a great silage pit for his grass crop, and an up-to-the-minute planned farmstead in which to display all this inventiveness.

With an almost virgin farm landscape to develop in the eighteenth century, Northumberland was a fertile county for new ideas. It was no accident that Daniel Garrett's pattern book of 1747, the very first for farmhouse and buildings of the farmstead, should be directed to the landowners of that part of the country. Arthur Young, late in the eighteenth century, reported that at least 600,000 acres of the county (over half its area) were wasteland, but by the early nineteenth century money made in trade and industry was pouring into the land.

Northumberland farmers were able, like those of Devon and Cornwall, to take advantage of local industrial expertise. The mines of the district (and they were spread throughout the farmland) suggested mechanisms for powering the farmstead. Wheel-houses to protect the horse-wheel can be found all over the area and the lofty engine-house

Overleaf: A rare survival of a Welsh longhouse in which only a door separated farmer and animals – Llanerch y Cawr, Elan Valley.

Right: Pastoral farming at Troutbeck, Cumbria. The farm was given by Beatrix Potter to the National Trust.

220

chimneys of later steam-powered machinery are also part of the rural landscape.

Some farms built in the Victorian period are almost villages in themselves. Not only do they present an astonishing arrangement of linked buildings for the functions of the farm but they also provided housing for labourers. Often they were mean, single-storey terraced cottages (much commented upon by observers as sub-standard and little better than the housing given to the animals of the farm), grouped around the farmstead. This arrangement had much in common with the medieval or feudal one where the servants lived within the wings of the great fortified complex for additional security. In the Victorian era, however, the farm cottages were linked to the farmstead for convenience rather than for defence; in other areas of England there was usually village housing of some description for labourers but Northumberland, so battered from centuries of civil disorder and military incursion, had little of the kind to offer them. These miserable tied cottages kept the work force handy, in a system of 'bondage' on the lines of medieval manorial practice.

Local detail

The dominant building material of these northern parts is stone of various types, with slate for roofs. On the eastern coast, and on the lowland dairy farms of Durham, tiling with rich red pantiles is a link with the farms of Yorkshire, Lincolnshire and Norfolk.

Detail plays an important part in the appearance of the northern farmstead. The pentice canopy, the tiled overhang which runs along both barn and farmhouse in the Lake District, is a practical measure providing shelter. It also functions as an architectural feature – a kind of string course binding the buildings together. The so-called spinning gallery, a rarity, seems to have been provided as an airing space, and perhaps a working one too. The pitched outshuts and ventilation slits

further break up what would otherwise be bulky, box-like structures. Again, they combine function with visual appeal. Crow-stepped gables, cylindrical chimneys and dated lintel-stones are added to farmhouses, and as the domestic quarters move up the social scale the architectural detail becomes more sophisticated. The grander farmhouses of Westmorland (now in Cumbria) are a far cry from the laithe-house, and its ancestor the longhouse.

Detail on the model farmsteads of the North East is more specifically that of architectural fashion of a given moment. It includes classical arcading and fake arrow slits on early nineteenth-century farms at Alnwick, Gothic finials and nineteenth-century 'Tudor' drip-moulds on later designs.

With so much stone, the northern counties have lost fewer of their farm buildings through sheer disintegration. However, particularly for the more remote farms, such as those seen perching seductively high above the Lakeland valleys, modern pressures are taking their toll on the farm buildings. The farmer wishes to live in or near the village; perhaps one or two small farms have amalgamated leaving at least one farmhouse redundant, with the buildings crumbling from lack of maintenance. Although the farmer might be able to sell it off as a holiday home, or rent it out, the buildings have to be repaired with care and with proper materials (a large part of this area is National Park). Factors such as these put uneven pressures on agriculture. As the experience of the National Trust, large landowners in the Lake District and, indeed, all over the northern counties, shows, the proper treatment and replacement of buildings cannot be supported financially at this level of farming. (The National Trust's works here are subsidized by their estates elsewhere.)

In a region where farming has never been easy, new problems are being faced – to a large extent the increase in tourism has dictated that the landscape remains unchanged, buildings and all, and the farmer has insufficient funds to meet the necessary stringent planning controls. The cost of special materials required in the circumstances should, many feel, be fully met from grant aid – a public contribution *pro bono publico*.

Above left: Ivy-clad farmhouse and attached farm buildings near Cambo, Northumberland. The arcaded building on the right of the picture is a cart-shed.

Left: Dyke Head farm, built in the 1840s, on the Wallington estate – an unusually small-scale model farm arranged around a yard.

Right: The hemmel was a Northumbrian traditional shelter for sheep or cattle, here part of the architect-designed agricultural estate of the Duke of Northumberland (*c.* 1830).

Far right: Purpose-built livestock sheds and yards at East Brizlee Farm in Alnwick Castle park, Northumberland.

Wales

The agricultural landscape of Wales today is over-whelmingly pastoral – a rolling landscape of small green fields, thickly hedged in the valleys and stone-walled on the hillsides. It is clearly the landscape of a wet climate, with lush pastures and hedges which keep the livestock within their allotted patch. Formerly, however, a very great quantity of grain was grown, both in the upland areas (almost 60 per cent of Wales is at least 500 ft above sea-level) and in the broad, fertile valleys and coastal lowlands. For the hill farmers, the grain was largely for their own domestic use, and for feeding the stock in winter, but for the lowland farmers it was an important cash crop. Defoe reports 'great quantities of corn' being exported from Chepstow and Newport, supplies coming from the Wye and Usk valleys respectively, bound for Portugal and elsewhere. 'Considering the mountainous parts of the west of this country, 'tis much they should have such good corn and so much of it to spare,' he wrote in the early 1700s.

From Tudor times, Wales had begun to experience stability and prosperity, and farmers had built upon the potential of the country to a remarkable degree. Enclosure had come early to Wales, as to other western regions. Welsh farmers had specialized their agricultural activity in ways which held good until the nineteenth century. Defoe also noted the dairying activities of the southern low-

Trecastle, near Brecon, Powys.

lands (supplying butter to Bristol and even to Spain) as well as the cattle rearing which took place on the inhospitable mountains and moors.

On these hardy black cattle a great deal of the farmer's fortune depended. They were driven along the drovers' roads to England, and fattened for sale *en route*, on the rich lowland pasture of the border counties or even much further away, in Kent for example. The importance of this trade was such that the drover played a central role in life in these parts – carrying with him the livelihood of a large number of small tenant farmers, including their cash in an early version of a banking system.

The buildings of the farm

As far as the built landscape of the farm is concerned, the east side of the country showed a greater susceptibility to change and influence than the western regions, which were always some way behind. The border areas, the Severn valley and the northern lowlands benefited from the English building boom which had begun in the late sixteenth century. Coinciding with the post-Tudor tranquillity in Wales, the new rich merchants began to invest in land and to build impressive houses often as the centre of a manorial farmstead. Where they were close to the English counties, they were timber-framed, the cruck frame system being largely replaced by post and truss. Elsewhere they were built of brick or high quality stone. These farmsteads included sizable corn barns as well as accommodation for cattle and oxen. In addition, the fine buildings suggested new patterns for the smaller-scale farmhouse and its buildings that were to follow.

Further west, the dates for the dominant re-building period become more and more recent. In Carmarthenshire, for example, where a shift towards more efficient and intensive dairying in the nineteenth century called for more systematic planning of the farmstead, the built landscape is largely of that date, although in terms of design, the houses are literally in the style of the late eighteenth century.

Group of farm buildings at Mathafarn, Machynlleth – the slatted opening in the outshut was replaced in more sophisticated farms with half-glazed or half-louvred windows.

Right: The farmyard in winter
at Llandefalle, Powys. The
arcaded building (centre of
picture) is a cart-shed.

Right: The 19th-century farmhouse at Llandefalle adjoins the cart-shed. It is large by the usual Welsh farmhouse standards.

Below: Interior of the barn at the same farm – the windows are probably a later addition, installed when the building became a cow-byre.

The more elaborate features of Victorian design passed Wales by. The Welsh dairy farmer continued to build a solid two-storey house, two rooms deep, with a small porch and perhaps an attic storey for the labourers. If more space was needed he added a bay each side and took the service areas round to a wing at the back. Stone-built, with a slate roof, the house was sometimes colour-washed, the green landscape being punctuated at intervals with a dash of white or pink. The pastoral farming and an easy supply of both stone and slate has led to a surprising uniformity in the rural buildings of Wales, both in scale and materials.

The main variations lay in the treatment of the materials. In Snowdonia, for example, great boulders were pressed into service, for both house and outbuildings, and for walling. Some of these immense stones date back to early Celtic farms. (Wales bears many traces of Celtic agriculture.) Other variations, such as the cylindrical chimneys of some farmhouses on the St. David's peninsula in Pembrokeshire, or localized versions of fashionable details, show small regional shifts in style but do not interrupt the overall homogeneity of forms and material.

The rebuilding and overbuilding that has occurred does mean that much of the farm is likely to be of later date than it appears.

Livestock buildings

Cattle, once the principal resource of the Welsh farmer, required housing, whether the hardy breeding stock or dairy herds. The practice of transhumance – the move to summer pasture and the 'hafod' (the Welsh word for the upland house) – meant that two sets of buildings were required. The practice continued in Wales long after it died out in other upland areas of Britain and ended only when sheep replaced cattle, and close supervision of the animals was no longer necessary.

A combination of practical and social motives seems to have prompted the practice of removing to the upper pastures. According to Peter Smith, the pre-enclosure need to remove livestock from open arable areas was the practical determinant, while the pleasure of removing to clean, fresh quarters perhaps explained the social motivation to move house annually. Double provision meant that both sets of buildings were rudimentary, often giving a single roof for the shelter of both humans and animals in the form of the longhouse. Sometimes the upland farm became the permanent farmstead after the annual migration ceased.

The cow-byre in this region, whether contiguous to the farmhouse, or standing separate from it across the yard, had been a simple, single-storey structure. Development of a second storey allowed for the storage of hay. The cow-byres in the fields were constructed on the same principle and, like their Yorkshire counterparts, made use of the change of level to let hay in above, while the cattle entered from below; the hay could then be pushed down to them as required.

Purpose-built accommodation for hay was developed as quantities increased and since, unlike straw, there were no processing activities associated with the crop, a simple post and lintel structure evolved. These variants of the Dutch barn consisted of a roof, usually slated, and supports of brick, stone or, near the Dolgellau slate quarries, great fingers of slate. Sometimes the barns were grouped in the farmstead area; sometimes they stood out in the fields.

Following the eighteenth- and nineteenth-century publications of the agricultural improvers, farmyard design was formalized into a central fold-yard surrounded by ranges of buildings. The larger farms expanded this pattern, introducing further yards and additional complexities to the layout. In North Wales and some of the Welsh border counties, English landowners imported ideas for farmsteads tried out on their estates elsewhere. Fashionable model farms here followed the same pattern as those built from Yorkshire to Surrey.

However, even the smallest pastoral farms shared the plan of the central foldyard, surrounded by single-storey calf-stalls (or 'hulls') and byres which could be used for indoor feeding during winter months as well as for milking. The dairy was, obviously, an important part of this arrangement, sometimes in a separate building or, more often, incorporated into the farmhouse. Most small farmers also kept a pig or two, which lived off the by-products of the dairy; one pig was killed around

Brick-built granary above stables at Meifod, Powys. The conveyor belt has made the stairs redundant.

January for a meat supply through the latter months of winter, while a second was fattened for sale. By the late nineteenth century, small dairies replaced the farm-based ones, and these, in turn, were superseded by centralized marketing, manufacture and collection.

By the turn of the twentieth century, the emphasis had shifted from breeding cattle to the running of hardy moorland sheep. In built terms, this had little effect on the farmstead. Apart from shelter walls, sheep need little purpose-built accommodation, and any spare cattle sheds could be adapted simply for storage space.

Sheep produced their own occasions in the rural calendar; sheep shearing, like threshing time, has always been a feverish time with its own rituals. The markets where stock was, and still is, bought and sold have remained important social occasions – few farmers, even today, turn down the chance to go to market once a week.

As far as the general impact of the farm buildings on the Welsh landscape is concerned, the instinctive use of materials and choice of site seem to have eluded the modern Welsh farmer – sometimes to a more disastrous degree than his English counterpart. Some of Wales has been badly scarred within

the last fifteen years – despite a legacy of beautiful buildings (in aggregate rather than individually) lasting some 300 years. Of course, the splendid natural landscape has introduced its own problems, as in the Lake District and in the West Country. Farmland is more profitably engaged in housing caravans than pasturing sheep; farmhouses and buildings are potential gold-mines if they can be turned into short-let holiday accommodation. The imbalance is bound to occur, but unfortunately planning controls have been badly applied over much of Wales, so that these developments tend to have the maximum impact.

Countrywide, the only exemptions to the very tight rein kept on new developments outside the village have been the houses built for farm workers. Thus a rash of ill-designed new farmhouses and bungalows dot the countryside, financed by generous grants. Many of these sit, literally, on the doorstep of an older house, rendering it physically unusable. There is, in addition, a particular clause in planning which exchanges the permission to build a new house for an undertaking not to use the old one. That agreement has been the death-knell to many a fascinating building – especially those masked by later alterations.

Below: An extensive 19th-century cattle yard at Mathrafal, Powys, built to cope with a large herd. Yards as large as this one are, of course, a post-Agricultural Revolution phenomenon. Before that the shortage of winter fodder made it impossible for farmers to over-winter large herds.

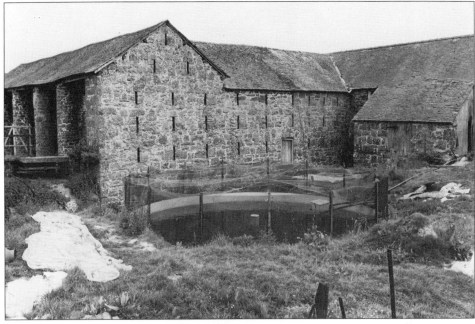

Above: The farm pond at Mathrafal with a Dutch barn of similar construction to many in the southern counties of England.

Left: The interior of the Dutch barn. The regular ventilation slits ornament an otherwise sternly functional building.

Above: Farm landscape near
Machynlleth, Powys. Barn,
cow-byre and Dutch barn line
up to one side of the
farmhouses.

Right: Outstanding example of
timber-framed and brick-
nogged farm buildings in the
Meifod Valley. Border
traditions dominate here, owing
to the availability of brick and
timber. Further west stone and
slate are the common building
material.

Epilogue

If you accept that the large majority of traditional farm buildings are essential to the landscape, one question lingers: how, given the modern economic pressures on agriculture, can the remaining ones realistically survive?

The best solution is to keep the buildings in some form of farming use, even if not for the purpose for which they were originally designed. Although the true function of the barn ceased with the introduction of the threshing machine, farmers have usually found it practicable since then to continue using barns for general storage. If a barn is very large (and most medieval timber-framed barns are vast), the problems of usage tend to be less, but those of maintenance are correspondingly larger. For a large barn, with great double doors, partial use for storage, whether of hay and straw, fodder, fertilizers or machinery and plant has always been a possibility – until now. As Essex County Council has pointed out, an aisled, timber-framed barn is not an ideal place to keep heavy, unmanoeuvrable machinery.[1] Nevertheless, for smaller implements it has always been quite suitable. Similarly, small grain dryers can be installed or sacks of nitrates stored there. For the important historic barn, the storage of highly inflammable fuels or hay and straw presents a danger, as was shown by the burning of the National Trust's Bredon Tithe Barn in Worcestershire during early 1980. There are other dangers, too, for the historically important farm building: making a new entrance or cutting into the timber-framed interior can also desecrate a fine structure. Such damage cannot be undone.

Remains of a once elegant set of farm buildings at North Aston, Oxfordshire. The iron ventilation shafts with their fancy 19th-century hoods are evidence of adaptation over the years.

However, ironically enough, some modern developments have worked to the advantage of old buildings. The fork-lift truck can turn in its own space within the posts of a great aisled barn. New high pressure blowers can cram grain into bins in the corners and sides of structurally delicate buildings without endangering the structure. Drying equipment for hay can fit into a threshing barn without difficulty.

The smaller buildings of the farm usually have a better chance of survival. Most buildings between 16 and 20 ft wide can be converted into milking parlours; the placing of the animals and the methods of milking may be radically changed but a sound building of the right measurements is often as good as, and cheaper than, a new structure. Sometimes an old cattle shed has been turned to this purpose, with an adjacent barn used as a collecting space for the animals, which are then sent down to the milking parlour itself.

Rarer building types can survive into a new use too, such as the Victorian silage pit, which now makes a perfect grain store, or the engine-house, which has been turned into a neat little implement shed or workshop.

Small buildings, with their insulation provided by the natural materials of traditional construction, brick, stone or weather-boarding, are also ideal for the raising of young animals. The condensation problems caused by asbestos roofing are notoriously bad, and calves are very vulnerable to pneumonia.

Almost no official attention is paid to the subject of conversion of farm buildings to new uses within agriculture. The Ministry figure of £333 million expenditure during 1979 on farm buildings and equipment (fixtures associated with the buildings) does not break down the figure between new buildings, repair, conversion or maintenance. The excellent Farm Buildings Information Centre library has just one article in its file on the subject of agricultural conversions since 1970. A new award is being offered by the Country Landowners' Association in 1981, the Henley Award, specifically for the conversion of farm buildings (to any use) and this may be seen as symptomatic of the stirrings of interest in the problem as a whole.

If the farmstead is listed, the farmer is compelled to seek permission to demolish it. (He can of course 'demolish by default', by letting the buildings fall into ruins, but his local council is empowered to take action against such neglect.) A listed farm building, or farmstead, can be repaired or maintained with loans or grants from the various appropriate sources – local or county authorities and local and national historic buildings trusts.

However, precious few farm buildings *are* listed. The Montagu Report on the re-use of historic buildings points out, in the section devoted to farm buildings, that, apart from medieval tithe barns (listed Grade 1, Grade 2★ or 2, or protected as Ancient Monuments), listing as a means of protection hardly touches the farm.[2] The first round of listing, between 1947 and 1967, concentrated on country houses and village nuclei; since then urban areas have attracted the attention of the resurvey team (in any case now pitifully thin and over-stretched). The report states *As a result, the vast majority of architecturally or historically interesting farm buildings remain unidentified and unprotected*' (the italics are those of the report).

The importance of buildings within the landscape is not one of the criteria for official listing, although in built-up areas this criterion applies for designating a Conservation Area. Very few farm buildings are individual gems and most farmsteads have to be considered as a whole; barns are freqently just one feature within a complete farmyard setting and to consider them separately could be an error – a single preserved barn, once divorced from its original setting, does not have much point. The Montagu Report suggests that finance is not the only sticking point in the problem of farm buildings – planning policies vary widely across the country and therein lies much of the trouble. Where finance is concerned, it suggests an arrangement comparable to that offered in many historic towns – the so-called Town Scheme in which the Department of the Environment (through the Historic Buildings Council), the county and the local authorities are equal partners in providing grant aid in deserving cases.

Nor is it just conservationists who envisage older farm buildings remaining in use, important within modern farming and the historic landscape. *Farmer's Weekly*, not overly sentimental in these matters, stated: '. . . few would deny their contribution to the atmosphere of stability and continuity which is part of the rural scene . . . . If they are used then there is a far better chance that they will be maintained in good condition and will continue to enhance the environment.'[3]

A useful future for existing farm buildings is rarely the concern of the officers of the Agricultural Development and Advice Service (ADAS) of the Ministry of Agriculture, although an improvement in new design is recognized as necessary there too.[4] If conversion of an existing building to new farming use increases productivity, then it falls within a category for which Ministry of Agriculture grants are available – otherwise it comes under the province of the Department of the Environment. This compartmentalization is a major problem in all areas of Government policy, not merely in the case of historic farm buildings. The EEC directives which might conceivably apply to the repair of farm buildings have not been followed up by the British Government, in contrast to policy in other member countries.[5] In France, the Ministry of Agriculture is also responsible for 'rural development'. This colours their attitude to the use of farm buildings to assist employment, outside agriculture – in tourism the *gîte* system of farmhouse holidays is one such example.

Conversion to new uses is a complicated subject – too lengthy to dwell on here.[6] The quality of the conversion is usually the key to success and many barns have been converted into houses without jarring the landscape or losing the major features of the original building. Unfortunately, the good examples are many times outnumbered by ill-considered conversions in which knick-knackery drives out every worthwhile characteristic of the building. Some converted barns would have been better demolished.

Many of the farm buildings that have fallen out of use have done so for reasons that equally bedevil their potential for re-use. Chief among these is inaccessibility. Even this can occasionally be turned to good account. The little, stone field barns of the Pennines, out on the hillside far from either track or road, much less main services, might seem to be fated. Yet, in various places, schemes have been set up to convert them into rudimentary over-night shelters for long-distance walkers. For this use they are in exactly the right place, and if the relaxation of rigorous fire and health standards is obtained, they can be 'converted' at very little cost and with no outward alteration to the fabric.

There is perhaps more hope for the re-use of some derelict farm buildings in the present economic climate than there has been for some time. Considerable money and energy are being spent on the development of small workshop-based industries in the counties to stem rural depopulation and deprivation. New 'high technology' industries using small components and dependent on electronic communications do not need to be sited in the city or already industrialized areas. Their flexibility may prove to be a major force in the reinvigoration of the countryside, benefiting both people and buildings. Former farm buildings could serve a useful purpose and the Council for Small Industries in Rural Areas is exploring the possibilities together with other countryside organizations (the National Farmers' Union and the Country Landowners' Association, for example). Other ideas such as community use, farm museums or farm shops can also bring a local landmark (perhaps of no outstanding architectural or historical significance) back into the life of its area, and preserve it within the landscape.

It requires constant vigilance to keep old farm buildings standing. Once a few slates or tiles are lost, it is a short step to losing the roof and, after that, the walls. The costs of maintenance are not prohibitive. But the Ministry of Agriculture, has just one booklet on the subject, and even that has been out of print for a number of years. A strong corrugated iron roof will keep a fine timber-framed building dry but a disintegrating thatched roof will allow it to rot away. Better a roughly patched-up building than one half-way to dereliction. Surprisingly, despite figures that showed, for example, that in Berkshire in 1968 a third of all existing farm buildings had been built since 1957, in the country as a whole two-thirds of farm buildings are pre-1957 (the year in which the Government Farm Improvement Scheme, the first of a series of grants towards farm buildings, was introduced). Of these, half the buildings are pre-1914. This means that most farmers do have to maintain old buildings; yet if a farmer neglects an historic barn and a subsequent owner wishes to repair it for agricultural use, the present grant scheme does not allow him any allocation.

Where buildings have disintegrated it is obviously important that the traditional materials should not be wasted. Yet this introduces a 'Catch 22' dilemma. Salvaged materials can give life to existing buildings but if they assume too high a value on their own account, then barns and farm buildings will be demolished in order to capitalize on that market. It provides another argument in favour of better listing; at least (in principle) a listed building cannot disappear overnight.

Many sets of vernacular buildings stand in the shadow of new buildings, which are often closer to warehouses in type (hence the term 'umbrella' shed) and more suited to the urban industrial estate than to the countryside. The scale of operation on the farm is always increasing. Between 1975 and 1979 dairy herd sizes went up by an average 25 per cent. No planning permission at all is needed for new farm buildings under 5,000 sq ft that are a certain distance from roads or housing; many monstrosities have arisen, generously funded by the grant system. The present Farm Capital Grant Scheme, dating from 1973, offers, at the time of writing, grants of between 20 and 30 per cent on capital works; grants in recent years have risen as high as 40 per cent.

In areas designated as 'of particular landscape beauty' safeguarding controls exist. The use of traditional materials is encouraged, as well as suitable colouring in 'new' materials, but no coherent effort is made to defray the costs to the farmer. (These are almost inevitably the less affluent, hill farming districts.)

Although there is a wealth of information on the design and construction of farm buildings (design guides, published competition designs and County Council planning department publications), atrocious buildings still appear.[7] Architects and other appropriate professionals, chartered surveyors or engineers, are rarely employed to design, plan and site new farm buildings. The whole business is usually left in the hands of the farmer, who buys the structure from a catalogue or advertisement, as a package deal. Modern farm buildings do not indicate a very impressive standard of design education or public awareness in this country. The only comfort is that most modern buildings are expendable. With the change of emphasis in agriculture moving so fast, many new farm buildings do not have a very long life expectancy.[8]

Derelict field barn in Gloucestershire, a familiar enough scene. Outlying buildings stand least chance of finding a new use once they become redundant and are often swiftly plundered for materials. Once the roof has gone, the building will disappear at surprising speed.

Now that the farm office has moved closer to the doctor's surgery, with its heaps of leaflets and technical literature, it is perhaps not surprising that the great corn stores and shelter sheds of modern farming should be indistinguishable from a factory unit on an industrial estate. Some of them are impressive structures, which give new emphasis to the landscape. There *are* examples of farm buildings winning architectural awards but they are rare gems. Not all that is new is bad![9]

In a recent article in the *Farm Buildings Digest* some winds of change were detected: 'Farmers will not be able to afford to have bigger and newer buildings than their neighbour primarily for prestige but hopefully they will seek good design, sound buildings and a long structural life . . . buildings that will be an asset to the farm, attractively designed, well maintained and flexible rather than buildings for the economist.' In short, few but better new buildings may be the picture in the future.

However, agriculture is not immune from the energy crisis: new farm buildings may well be closer to their traditional predecessors than to the controlled environments of recent 'innovatory' building; the older farm buildings may well come into their own. There will also be new, specially designed structures, responsive to new technologies, and a change of emphasis which will certainly affect the farmer just as much as the householder or industrialist. It is doubly important that farmers know how to use or re-use them, how to finance their maintenance and repair and, perhaps above all, that they understand why they were built as they were, and the farming lore and good commonsense that went into their construction.

Most recent writers on farm buildings have unquestioningly written off the legacy of the past. The idea seems to be that provided the structures are archaeologically recorded, then they can be allowed to disappear. Important though that factor may be, it seems to miss the point. In the cities, towns and villages a terrible lesson has been learnt; if the fine buildings of the past are not defended, someone, somewhere, will find a good reason to remove them. In the urban context, the lesson is almost learnt and the economic recession has done the rest but, in the countryside, this is not so. Where listing is so inadequate and where investment returns are as closely guarded as in the City, short-term financial gain must not spell the long-term desecration of the landscape.[10] Conservation of buildings is often sound financial sense in any case. Moreover, the landscape does not belong to us alone. In the introduction, this book was claimed as a celebration; it would be a tragedy if it were to be an epitaph.

The National Trust and Farms

Farmhouses and farmland inevitably form part of the great estates and large tracts of countryside which come under the protection of the National Trust. These farms are let to tenant farmers and the income from farm rents produces a contribution to the Trust's finances. But because so much of the Trust's agricultural holdings are spread across the uplands of Wales, the Lake District, the Peak District and other areas of low productivity, where practically the only possible land-use, apart from afforestation, is sheep farming, the income received from the Trust's half million acres is not as substantial as might at first be expected.

National Trust farm rents are kept under constant review, and in general they are in step with rents on comparable farms not owned by the Trust. It is not possible to put a precise figure on the number of National Trust farms, since it is hard to define precisely what constitutes a farm. There are certainly well over one thousand holdings.

Apart from the value of their contribution to the Trust's finances, farm buildings and land form a precious reservoir of vernacular buildings and wildlife refuges. The Trust regards both as of great importance in its work as its more widely advertised concern for great houses and fine gardens. Its responsibility for the preservation of smaller buildings, which reflect a long tradition of building with local materials under local conditions, is taken seriously, for it is here, rather than in the mansions of the wealthy, that continuity of style and purpose can best be appreciated. Similarly, when so much agricultural land has fallen to the plough, the Trust tries to keep enclaves of wilderness on its farms where wildlife has a chance of survival.

Farming, as Gillian Darley so clearly shows, has changed greatly in the lowlands over the past fifty years; yet, as she equally clearly demonstrates, farmers have in the past been marvellously ingenious in the ways they have adapted old buildings to new uses. The Trust believes that in many cases there is no need for farm buildings to be destroyed or to become derelict; nor is there often any excuse for unsympathetic additions or conversions which are out of tune with the regional traditions. In a few cases, however, the erection of inexpensive prefabricated buildings, or the destruction of those which have outlived their function, is the only logical solution.

While fully aware of the needs of modern intensive farming, the National Trust has safeguarded, to the best of its ability, the character and lives of its farm buildings and farmland.

Robin Wright, April 1981.

Blickling, Norfolk.

Notes to the Text

Introduction

1 The grants have had various names and have varied in their percentage allocation over the years. At present the capital grants available for farmers are the Farm and Horticultural Development Scheme, and the Farm Capital Grant Scheme, 1973. Grants are increased for hill farming areas (in EEC parlance, Less Favoured Areas – a rather wider category).

2 *English Cottages and Farmhouses* by Olive Cook with photographs by Edwin Smith, Thames and Hudson, 1954.

The Landscape

1 *Fields, Hedges and Ditches* (Shire Publications), 1976.

2 W.G. Hoskins, *History from the Farm* (Faber and Faber), 1970: a collection of articles, based on entries to a competition in *Farmer's Weekly* in 1968. See also M. Beresford, *The Lost Villages of England* (Lutterworth Press), 1954.

3 Explained more fully in *Cambridge Agrarian History*, Vol. IV, Ch. 1, Section A.

4 *Cambridge Agrarian History*, Vol. IV, 'Enclosing and engrossing'.

5 The Board of Agriculture reports on the agriculture of the English counties were published throughout the Board's existence from 1793 until 1815: some of the earlier reports were reissued in revised form during this period.

6 *The Making of the English Landscape* Hodder, 1955.

The Site and Plan of the Farm

1 A.D. Hall in *A Pilgrimage of British Farming, 1910–1912*, John Murray, 1913, refers to the 'strange reticulation of crops in narrow strips' to be seen in the Isle of Axholme just before World War I. It was 'a little bit of country that has been left as a kind of outlier in time, to report to the 20th century on the manner of land-holding of our remotest forefathers'. The area still practised open field farming then, as Laxton in Nottinghamshire does to this day.

2 See Flora Thompson's *Lark Rise* (OUP), 1954.

3 His inventions made slow headway because it was difficult and expensive to get machines made, and because their use was largely limited to light soils.

4 Machine-breaking was reported as early as 1815 in Suffolk and continued as an expression of the frustrations and miseries of the rural poor until the crescendo of fury of 1830. Some farmers broke their own machines rather than suffer attack by labourers. Harsh penalties were meted out to offenders which helped to crush the opposition to machinery. The organisation of labour into unions in the 1870s turned the spotlight on the hardships suffered by the agricultural labour force. *See* P. Horn, *The Rural World, 1780–1850: Social Change in the English Countryside*, Hutchinson, 1980.

5 The term 'model' farm has both architectural and agricultural connotations. Advanced farms were usually housed in conditions as near to the ideal as possible, hence the buildings and the methods of husbandry were usually equally advanced.

6 H. Stephens' *The Book of the Farm* (several editions were published from 1844 onwards in London and Edinburgh) is full of such curious devices.

7 The Royal Commission on Agricultural Depression, was also known as the Duke of Richmond's Commission. It sat between 1879 and 1882 and among its recommendations called for the appointment of a Minister of Agriculture. This was implemented in 1889. A second Royal Commission in 1893 found that the first depression had eked away all available resources and that landowners and farmers had no further reserves to meet the continued downturn. In the period between the two commissions, the value of farm produce in the nation had almost halved, while costs had continued to rise.

8 Christopher Hussey in an article entitled 'Outbuildings at Barrington Court, Somerset' in *Country Life*, September 8, 1928 thought the farm showed 'foresight and largeness of ideas that is rarely met with nowadays in landed proprietors whether longseated or newly come'.

Materials and Construction

1 A straightforward guide, in a clear, brief format, is R. Harris's *Discovering Timber-framed Buildings*, Shire Publications, 1978.

2 The aisled barn allowed for considerable extra space to either side of the main area while the hammer-beam roof allowed for the span (on a cantilever principle) without the disadvantages of a series of posts, as required by an aisled structure.

3 Examples included the engravings of Knyff, and such paintings as the fine series by John Harris of Dunham Massey, the house and its surroundings.

4 *See* Gertrude Jekyll's *Old English Household Life*, Batsford, 1925. For the Victorian fixtures and fittings, see the article by S. Wade-Martin, 'Factory farming in the 1850s', *Country Life*, July 6, 1978. It is about the Egmere farm on the Holkham estate, built in the 1850s.

The Farmhouse

1 The observations of contemporary observers, such as Lambarde, were compiled in Fisher and Jurica's *Documents in English Economic History*, 'England from AD 1000 to 1760' Subsection 24 and 26, Bell, 1977.

2 See also *The Lake District: an Anthology*, edited by N. Nicholson, Hale, 1977, in which he quotes Wordsworth, writing in 1810 of 'a perfect Republic of Shepherds and Agriculturists, among whom the plough of each man was confined to the maintenance of his own family . . . the land, which they walked over and tilled had for more than five hundred years been possessed by men of their name and blood'. Harriet Martineau is also included in the same anthology. By 1855 she had chronicled the decline of the statesman as with 'no agricultural science and little skill' he was unable to compete with industrialization.

3 Architectural drawing in the Soane Museum, Lincoln's Inn Fields, London.

4 John Martin Robinson's article 'Estate Buildings at Holkham', *Country Life*, November 21 and 28, 1974.

5 Arthur Young 'A Week in Norfolk' (1792).

6 The subject is treated fully in J. Burnett's *A Social History of Housing: 1815–1970*, David and Charles, 1978. For improved estate cottages within planned villages see G. Darley's *Villages of Vision*, Paladin, 1978.

7 Corn Laws, which served as protection against cheap foreign imports, were opposed by Whigs and Radicals.
Sir Robert Peel's Government pinned its faith on the effect of improved methods on agriculture carried out in a free market and repealed the laws. This, allied to other favourable circumstances, led to a golden age in British farming although it was a setback in principle for the Conservative landed interest.

8 The system, a discretionary one, dreamed up to benefit the poor by guaranteeing a minimum wage, instead acted against their interests. Being a rigid system it held down their wages for over 30 years, and lead to the migration of labourers from the areas in which it was practised to those in which it was not. (*See* Horn, *op. cit.*).

Notes to the text

The Farm Buildings From Tradition to Innovation

1 F.W. Steer, *Farm and cottage inventories of mid-Essex, 1635–1749*, Phillimore, 1969, and those given in M.W. Barley's *The English Farmhouse and Cottage*, Routledge, 1961.

2 John Evelyn (1620–1706) was astonishingly active in a wide variety of fields; his agricultural knowledge came from his Continental travels during the Commonwealth period.

3 The bounties benefited the farmer, not the corn merchant, and were operated in tandem with a restriction on imported grain.

4 The agricultural depression was brought about by a combination of disastrous seasons and the flooding of the market by supplies from the colonies which undercut the British farmer. (*See* also Chapter 2, note 7.)

5 See the *Handbook to Cogges* edited by J.M. Steane, Oxfordshire County Council, 1980.

6 J.E.C. Peters, *The development of farm buildings in west lowland Staffordshire up to 1880*, Manchester University Press, 1969.

7 Innet Homes, 'Agricultural use of the Herefordshire house and its outbuildings,' *Vernacular Architecture*, Vol. 9, 1978.

8 *Thomas Tusser . . . his Good Points of Husbandry*, collated and edited by Dorothy Hartley (1931).

9 Described in *Traditional Kent Buildings, No. 1*, 1980, edited by Jane Wade: a series of studies by students at the School of Architecture, Canterbury College of Art.

10 D. Dymond, 'A 15th century building contract from Suffolk', *Vernacular Architecture*, Vol. 9, 1978.

The Farm Buildings – Change and Innovation

1 Ernle gives a full list of provincial agricultural societies in the late 18th and early 19th century in *English Farming, Past and Present*, Longmans, 1912.

2 Pusey's words are printed on the title page of Caird's *English Agriculture in 1850–51*, Longmans, 1852. (See also Biographical Notes.)

3 The Picturesque movement, based on an ideal landscape as portrayed by 17th century painters, was a curious amalgam of aesthetics and popular taste. It envisaged architecture as part of the whole – a moulded, perfect landscape. Thus farm buildings, as well as farmland, were often incorporated into schemes based more on popular fashion than on sound agricultural criteria.

4 P. de la Ruffinière du Prey, 'Oblivion for Soane's Cow barn?', *Country Life*, January 8, 1976.

5 Her farmyard, designed by Hubert Robert, was at the palace of Versailles and formed part of a rustic hamlet.

6 See M. Craig, *Classic Irish Houses*, Architectural Press, 1976. Arthur Young referred to 'gentlemen who farm for pleasure . . . I cannot see much use in men of large fortune applying in a common manner to farming'.

7 Thomas Whateley *Observations on Modern Gardening*, 1770.

8 John Carrington, a farmer himself, had already noted the process in his diary (*The Carrington Diary*, numerous editions). Writing in about 1799, he told of an old Hertfordshire farmer who was allowed to remain in his house (he was 79) but 'the land is to be laid to other farms'; the post-Napoleonic depression hastened the final decline of many such small farmers.

9 J.C. Loudon, *Encyclopaedia of Cottage, Farm and Villa Architecture*, Longmans, 1836 and revised editions.

10 William Marshall, *Planting and Rural Ornament, Vol. 1*, 1796.

11 Essay on threshing machines, *Georgical Essays*, 1804.

12 P.F. Robinson, *Designs for Farm Buildings*, London, 1830.

13 J.C.A. Voelcker (1822–84) was a German-born agricultural chemist who became Professor of Chemistry at the Royal Agricultural College, Cirencester in 1849 and Consultant Chemist to the Royal Agricultural Society in 1857. He published papers on many aspects of agriculture, but his name is particularly linked with his theories on manure.

14 G.T. Garratt, writing in *Hundred Acre Farm*, Longmans, 1928, put it as follows: 'The nation could spend £100,000 for the next few years and leave as much again to be done.'

Epilogue

1 See the Essex County Council publication, *The Essex Countryside: Historic Barns, a Planning Appraisal*, 1979.

2 *Britain's Historic Buildings: a policy for their future use*, British Tourist Authority, 1980.

3 Issue of January 9, 1976.

4 H.G. Penfold, 'Landscape and Farm Buildings', *ADAS Quarterly*, winter 1979.

5 The relevant directive, circular 75/268, article 1012, is considered too expensive in administration costs to be worth claiming.

6 However, the subject is coming up for increasingly wide discussion – for example see *New Uses for Redundant Farm Buildings*, November, 1980: the report of a seminar run by Hampshire County Council for Community Service and the County Planning Dept. See also the report following the working seminar organized by the 'Architects in Agriculture' Group, published as *Coleshill Model Farm, Oxfordshire: past, present, future*, 1981. The model farm studied was built in 1852 for the Earl of Radnor, the same estate as that visited by William Cobbett 30 years before. It now belongs to the National Trust.

7 For example, Cheshire County Council, as well as issuing a farm buildings' design guide also runs a 'Best Farm Buildings' competition adding, so to speak, carrot to stick. Only a handful of county authorities, however, are exemplary in their efforts in this direction.

8 The British Standard notice, 5502 (The code of practice for design of buildings and structures for agriculture), introduced in January 1, 1980, is classified according to categories which comprise a design life of between 50 and two years. The new standards have obvious implications on the design of farm buildings: no mention is made of the siting of buildings within the landscape.

9 The *Financial Times* Award for Industrial Architecture, 1971, went to the architects Scarlett Burkett Associates for their 60-cow dairy unit, for the Lee Abbey Fellowship in Devon. It was estimated that the buildings cost an extra £2,000 to meet aesthetic criteria.

10 See the prolonged correspondence in *The Times*, autumn 1980, prompted by Marion Shoard's *The Theft of the Countryside*, M.T. Smith, 1980. Curiously, hardly any letter writers mentioned the importance of historic or well-designed new buildings in the landscape.

Glossary

Aisled plan Timber-framing in which the main span of the building is separated by a range of timber posts and braces from the side aisles.

Ashlar Blocks of masonry worked to a smooth, even face and square edges.

Bastle (or bastel) Also referred to as a bastle- or bastel-house. A fortified farmhouse on the Scottish borders housing cattle below and humans above.

Bank barn Barn at first floor level, built on a slope, and entered at ground level or from a ramp, with a stable, cowshed or similar below.

Barton Devonshire term for the farmyard.

Bay Principal compartment of a building.

Box frame Form of timber-framing in which the roof trusses rest on a box-like structure of upright posts and horizontal beams.

Brick nogging Brick infill for walling of a timber-frame construction.

Catslide roof (see *Outshut*).

Chamfer Surface made when the square angle of a stone block is cut away, usually at an angle of 45° to the other two surfaces.

Clay bat (or lump) Large unfired bricks made of East Anglian clay used for building.

Clunch Hard chalk used as a building stone, particularly in Cambridgeshire.

Cob Clay mixed with straw, gravel and sand, and used as a walling material.

Cowl Covering over a chimney to improve ventilation, particularly on *oast houses*.

Crew yard (see *Foldyard*).

Cross-passage Passage that crosses from the front to the back of a house dividing domestic and service areas.

Cruck frame Timber framing using pairs of large curved timbers (or crucks) rising from ground level to the apex of the roof for the principal supports.

Double pile plan Farmhouse plan which allows for four rooms on two floors, two at the front and two at the back.

Drip-mould Projecting edge of a moulding, so channelled that rain falls easily away.

Dutch barn A simple post and lintel structure with open sides which ventilates yet covers the stored crop (usually hay).

Engine-house Feature of 19th-century farms, used to house a steam engine, and having a tall chimney.

Ferme ornée Parkland with elaborate farm buildings, not always a working farm.

Field barn Isolated cow house or shelter shed, usually with a loft over

Finial Decoration on top of a gatepost, gable or pinnacle.

Flemish bond Pattern used in bricklaying, with alternate *headers* and *stretchers* in every course.

Foil A lobe- or leaf-shaped decoration in stonework, hence trefoil (three lobes) and quatrefoil (four lobes).

Foldyard Open yard in which livestock is free to move about and produce manure, which is then distributed to the fields. A crewyard is the eastern term for it.

Gable Vertical wall at the end of a pitched roof, generally triangular. Dutch gables have curved outlines.

Gablet Small *gable* pierced to give ventilation.

Hafod Welsh term for a farmhouse on upper pastures used during annual removal of cattle to summer pasture on hill farms.

Hall house Medieval house with one large living room from floor to ceiling, with one or two service rooms off.

Hammer-beam A form of roof construction in which horizontal bracket usually projecting at wall-plate level is used to carry the arched braces and struts of the roof.

Header Brick placed with its length at right angles to the line of the wall.

Hemmel An arcaded shelter for sheep, traditional in Northumberland and (under another name) in Scotland. The space is often divided by a wall so that access can be gained from two separate fields.

High farming Victorian age of farming in which mechanization was fully exploited.

Hipped roof A roof with sloped, instead of vertical, ends.

Home farm The farm on a large estate farmed under direct surveillance of the landowner, often sited within the park itself.

Horse-wheel Horse-driven source of rotary power, used particularly for threshing.

Hull Alternative term for a loose-box, usually for calves.

Jetty Projecting floor joists supporting the overhang of a timber-framed building.

King post A perpendicular beam in the frame of a roof, rising from the *tie-beam* to the ridge.

Laithe-house A later version of the *longhouse* combining a house, barn and byre under one roof, with doors to each from the exterior.

Lath Narrow sliver of timber, used with plaster, for walling material.

Linhay Open-fronted upper-level hay barn with animal shelter below – a West Country building. The upper area is known as the 'tallet'.

Longhouse Farmhouse and byre beneath a single roof separated by a through-passage which usually serves as a common entry to both parts.

Louvre Slatted unglazed window for ventilation, often used in dairies.

Midden Collection place for manure within farmyard.

Midstrey Central entrance bay of a barn (strey = bay), with a projecting porch.

Nogging see *Brick nogging*.

Oast house Special structure built to house the kiln for drying hops.

Outshut Lean-to extension, roofed over by a catslide roof.

Pantiles Tiles made in an S-form, and thus easily overlapped, while preserving ventilation.

Pargetting Exterior plastering of timber-framed building, usually modelled in designs such as foliage or figures.

Pele tower Small fortified tower used in the Northern counties as defence against marauders, usually from Scotland.

Pentice canopy External protection at first-floor height provided by a narrow tiled jutting ledge – confined to wet regions.

Pisé Unfired bricks made of rammed earth, used when nearly dry.

Pitching eye (or hole) Opening in wall of barn or loft for unloading straw, corn or hay, usually closed with a sliding or hinged shutter.

Poundhouse West country building, purpose-built for the production of cider.

Queen post One of two upright posts, resting on the *tie-beam* and supporting the rafters.

Quoins Dressed stones laid at the corners of walls so that their faces are alternately large and small.

Rendering Plastering of outside walls, taking various forms.

Roughcast Type of coarse rendering.

Screens passage Passage from front to back of an open hall at the service end, separated by a screen from the main part of the hall.

Shieling North country version of the *hafod*.

Shingles Wooden roof tiles.

Shippon North country term for a cow-shed.

Staddle stones Mushroom-shaped stones used as a base to support timber-framed granaries or barns, to deter vermin.

Statesman North country term for a yeoman farmer.

Stretcher Brick placed with its length parallel to the line of the wall.

String course A projecting line of mouldings running horizontally along the face of a building.

Studs Upright timbers used in timber-framed houses.

Tallet See *Linhay*.

Threshing floor Hard surfaced transverse floor in a corn barn, used for threshing corn by hand.

Tie-beam Main horizontal beam connecting the base of rafters, to prevent them moving apart.

Tie-rod Metal member spanning the width of a building, tying the outside walls together.

Tile-hanging Exterior wall covering of overlapping rows of tiles, slates, or shingles.

Timber-framing Method of construction whereby principal supports for walls are timber struts laid vertically and horizontally with the spaces between filled by plaster or brickwork (known as nogging). Various types of timber frame exist, see also *Box frame* and *Cruck frame*.

Tithe barn Barn of exceptionally large dimensions in which the tithes (one tenth of the farm's produce) were stored – a levy paid to the clergy or ecclesiastical authorities.

Transhumance The annual removal of cattle to higher pastures during the summer months.

Wattle and daub Wall construction using braces and thin laths (wattles) interwoven and plastered over with mud or clay (daub).

Wealden house Medieval house originating in the South-east, it usually has an open hall in the middle and a two-storeyed bay at each end. The upper floors of the bays are jettied, usually to the front, sometimes to the side.

Weather-boarding Overlapping horizontal boards used as cladding for a building.

Wheel-house (or gin gang) Purpose-built structure for a large wheel, used to power threshing, either by water-, horse- or wind-power.

Bibliography

Contemporary travels
W. Camden, *Britannia*, 1586.

W. Cobbett, *Rural Rides*, 1830.

D. Defoe, *A Tour thro' the Whole Island of Great Britain*, 1724–7.

F. de la Rochefoucauld, *Frenchman in England*, 1784; translated edition, 1933.

C. Fiennes, *The Journeys of Celia Fiennes*, edited by Christopher Morris, Cresset Press, 1947.

P. Kalm, *Kalm's England*, 1748; translated edition, Macmillan, 1892.

H. Taine, *Notes on England*, 1872; translated edition, 1872

Diaries
N. Blundell, *Blundell's Diary and Letter Book, 1702–1728*, edited by Margaret Blundell, University Press, Liverpool, 1952.

J. Carrington, *The Carrington Diary*, edited by W.B. Johnson, 1956.

W. Cole, *The Blecheley Diary of the Rev. William Cole*, edited by F.G. Stokes, Constable and Co, 1931.

F. Kilvert, *Kilvert's Diary, 1870–1879*, edited by W. Plomer, Jonathan Cape, 1944.

J. Woodforde, *The Diary of a Country Parson, 1758–1802*, edited by J. Beresford, Oxford University Press, 1949.

Contemporary works including treatises, reports and pattern books.
Agriculture, Board of, *General View of the Agriculture of . . .* (series), 1793–1815.

R. Beatson, *On Farm Buildings*, 1796.

J. Burke, *British Husbandry*, 1834–1840 (4 volumes).

J. Caird, *English Agriculture 1850–51*, 1852.

J.B. Denton (editor), *The farm homesteads of England*, 1863

J. Fitzherbert, *The Boke of Husbandry*, 1523.

D. Garrett, *Designs and Estimates of Farmhouses*, 1747.

A.D. Hall, *A Pilgrimage of British Farming, 1910–1912*, John Murray, 1913.

W. Howitt, *The Rural Life of England*, 1840.

A. Hunter (editor), *Georgical Essays*, 1803.

N. Kent, *Hints to Gentlemen of Landed Property*, 1775.

T. Lightholer, *The Gentleman and Farmers' Architect*, 1774.

J.C. Loudon, *Encyclopaedia of cottage, farm and villa architecture, 1836* (and revised editions).

G. Markham, *The English Husbandman*, 1613.

W. Marshall, *Planting and Rural Ornament*, 1796 (2 volumes); *The Rural Economy of . . .* (series) 1798.

J. Plaw, *Ferme Ornée*, 1795.

P.F. Robinson, *Designs for Farm Buildings*, 1830.

H. Stephens, *The Book of the Farm*, 1844 – 3 volumes (and later revised editions).

T. Tusser, *Five hundred points of good husbandry, etc*, 1573.

C. Waistell, *Designs for Agriculture Buildings*, 1827.

J. Worlidge, *A Compleat System of Husbandry and Gardening*, 1713.

A. Young, Board of Agriculture reports (See *Agriculture* above). *The Farmer's Guide in hiring and stocking farms*, 1770 (2 volumes).

Twentieth-century references

Agriculture in Essex, 1840–1900, Essex Record Office, Pub. No. 67, 1975.

Arts Council exhibition catalogues, in particular: *English Cottages and Small Farmhouses*, by Paul Oliver; *Traditional Farm Buildings* by Richard Harris; and *Timber-framed Buildings*, also by Richard Harris.

M.W. Barley, *The English Farmhouse and Cottage*, Routledge, Keegan, Paul, 1961.

M. Beresford, *The Lost Villages of England*, Lutterworth Press, 1954.

R.W. Brunskill, *Illustrated Handbook of Vernacular Architecture*, Faber, 1978.

J. Burnett, *A Social History of Housing: 1815–1970*, Methuen, 1980.

Cambridge Agrarian History, Vol IV and Vol VIII, Cambridge University Press, 1967 and 1978.

A. Clifton-Taylor, *The Pattern of English Building*, Faber, 1972.

Ernle, Lord (as R.E. Prothero), *English Farming, Past and Present*, 1912.

D. Hartley, *The Land of England*, Macdonald and Jane, 1979.

N. Harvey, *History of Farm Buildings in England and Wales*, David and Charles, 1970. *The Industrial Archaeology of Farming in England and Wales*, Batsford, 1980.

E. Mercer, *English Vernacular Houses*, HMSO, 1975.

G.E. Mingay (editor), *The Agricultural Revolution: Changes in Agriculture 1750–1880*, Black, 1977.

Changes in Agriculture 1650–1880, Black, 1977.

J. & J. Penoyre, *Houses in the Landscape*, Faber, 1978.

John Martin Robinson, 'Model farm buildings in the Age of Improvement', *Architectural History*, Vol. 19, 1976.

Sir E.J. Russell, *History of Agricultural Science in Great Britain*, Allen & Unwin, 1966.

G.M. Trevelyan, *English Social History*, Longman, 1978.

Periodicals

Annals of Agriculture
Journal of the Royal Agricultural Society
Agricultural History Review
also articles in *Country Life, Industrial Archaeology* and other architectural periodicals.

Theses

John Popham: Farm Buildings, Function and Form. Submitted for Diploma in Conservation Studies, June 1973 (Institute of Advanced Architectural Studies, York).

Eileen Spiegel: The English Farm House: a Study of Architectural Theory and Design: doctoral thesis, 1960, Columbia University, New York.

Regional Bibliography

Certain sources have been used throughout this section. For the late 17th century, *The Journeys of Celia Fiennes*, Cresset Press, 1947 has been used. For the early 18th century, Daniel Defoe's *A Tour thro' the Whole Island of Great Britain*, 1724–7. For the late 18th and early 19th-century impressions, the County Reports of the Board of Agriculture, by Arthur Young and others, have been used, as well as the volumes on the *Rural Economy* (of various counties and areas – not countrywide) by William Marshall. For the mid-19th century, James Caird's *English Agriculture*, 1852, was the main source. Contemporary reference material comes from Vol. IV of the *Cambridge Agrarian History* and the volumes so far published of *The History of the Landscape*, edited by W.G. Hoskins and published by Hodder and Stoughton. Two useful bibliographies for detailed vernacular building studies, arranged region by region, are R. de Zouche Hall, *Bibliography on Vernacular Architecture*, 1972 and D. Michelmore, *A Current Bibliography of Vernacular Architecture, 1970–76*, Vernacular Architecture Group, 1979. Other reference material is listed below, region by region.

The South East

Traditional Kent Buildings, No. 1: studies by students at the School of Architecture, Canterbury College of Art. Edited by Jane Wade, published by the college, 1980.

The various Batsford publications on old cottages and farmhouses of these counties offer an excellent evocation of vernacular buildings as they stood at the turn of the century.

The Cotswolds and Southern Counties

Royal Commission on Historic Monuments, volumes on Dorset.

Edith Brill, *Life and Tradition in the Cotswolds*, Dent, 1973.

R. Wood-Jones, *Traditional Domestic Architecture of the Banbury Region*, Manchester University Press, 1963.

M.A. Havinden, *Estate Villages*, Reading University Press, 1966.

J.R. Gray, 'Industrial Farm Estate in Berkshire, *Industrial Archaeology*, Vol 8, 1971.

Architects in Agriculture Group – Occasional Paper No. 1. *Coleshill Model Farm: Past, Present, Future*, 1981.

The South West

Devon's Traditional Buildings, Devon County Council, 1978.

W.G. Hoskins, 'Some Old Devon Bartons', *Country Life*, September 22, 1950.

Bibliography

The Eastern Counties

Royal Commission on Historic Monuments – volumes on Cambridgeshire in particular those on the west, published in 1968, and the north-east, published in 1972.

The Essex Countryside: Historic Barns, a Planning Appraisal, Essex County Council, 1979.

C. Hewett, *Development of Carpentry, 1200–1900: an Essex study*, David and Charles, 1969.

The East Midlands and Humberside

T.H. Beastall, *The Agricultural Revolution in Lincolnshire*, Lincolnshire Local History Society, 1979.

A. Harris, *Rural Landscape of the East Riding of Yorkshire, 1700—1850*, OUP., 1961.

W.G. Hoskins, *Midland England*, Batsford, 1944. This account covers Bedfordshire and Huntingdon which are included in the Eastern counties chapter.

The West Midlands and Welsh Borders

J.E.C. Peters, *The development of farm buildings in west lowland Staffordshire up to 1800*, Manchester University Press, 1969.

John Martin Robinson, 'Remaking the Shugborough landscape', *Country Life*, March 10, 1977.

Innet Homes, 'Agricultural use of the Herefordshire house and its outbuildings', *Vernacular Architecture*, Vol. 9, 1978.

The Pennines and North-Eastern Uplands

M. Hartley and J. Ingilby, *Life and Tradition in the Yorkshire Dales*, Dent, 1968 and *Life in the Moorlands of North East Yorkshire*, Dent, 1972.

Anne and John K. Harrison, 'The horse wheel in North Yorkshire', *Industrial Archaeology*, Vol. 10, No. 3, 1973.

John Martin Robinson, 'In Pursuit of Excellence; farm buildings in the West Riding of Yorkshire, *Country Life*, June 28, 1979.

The Northern Borders

J. Brunskill, *Vernacular Architecture of the Lake Counties*, Faber, 1974.

J.H. Palmer, *Historic farmhouses in and around Westmorland*, Westmorland Gazette Ltd, revised edition, 1952.

H.G. Ramon, R.W. McDowall, Eric Mercer, *Shielings and Bastles*, Royal Commission on Historic Monuments, HMSO, 1970.

Wales

Peter Smith, *Houses of the Welsh Countryside*, HMSO, 1975.

Eyrwyn William, *Traditional farm buildings in Wales*, National Folk Museum of Wales, 1973 (with English summary).

Biographical Notes

Bakewell, Robert (1725–1795) Leicestershire livestock breeder who revolutionized agriculture by improving the existing strains of stock, producing new breeds of sheep, cattle and horse. He introduced a stud system and improved his pastures by deliberate periodic flooding. By good feeding and sound housing, as well as humane treatment of the animals – his sheep were 'kept as clean as racehorses and sometimes put into body-clothes' – he bred strains of animals immeasurably superior to any known before.

Caird, Sir James (1816–1892) Scottish farmer who was commissioned by *The Times* to report on the state of agriculture following the adoption of Free Trade, for which he had campaigned vigorously. Originally taking the form of letters to *The Times*, his report was published in book form by Longmans in 1852 as *English Agriculture in 1850–51*, the first such survey since the Board of Agriculture Reports fifty or more years before.

Cobbett, William (1763–1835) A farmer's son and a farmer himself, he was a Radical and a prolific polemicist. His commentaries on the state of the rural community in the early 19th century formed a savage indictment of Parliamentary Enclosure and the amalgamation of holdings. The *Rural Rides*, published in London in 1830 give a fine evocation of the countryside in the early 19th century as well as pinpointing the miseries of humble country people, in particular the independent small farmer.

Coke, Thomas William (1752–1842) was created Earl of Leicester in 1837. On inheriting the Holkham estate in Norfolk in 1776, he took an active part in farming, becoming the leading agricultural improver of his generation. He also fought for agriculture in the House of Commons (as a Whig). The famous Holkham Annual Sheep Shearings were an event in the agricultural calendar: Coke also introduced the widespread growing of wheat to north Norfolk and bred a strain of Suffolk pig, as well as Bakewell's Leicestershire sheep. His son, the second Earl, also called Thomas William (1822–1909) continued the tradition, farming the 40,000 acre estate in the most progressive manner of Victorian 'high farming': he was hit severely by the Agricultural Depression from the late 1870s onwards. He was a member of the second Royal Commission on Agriculture of 1893.

Kent, Nathaniel (1737–1816) A land valuer and agent he studied agriculture in the Netherlands, and then brought the fruits of his observations to bear on British farming. Publication of *Hints to Gentlemen of Landed Properties* in 1775 brought him much work on land management: he worked in Norfolk and was author of the Norfolk county report for the Board of Agriculture in 1794. For a while he was Bailiff to George III at Windsor and he also contributed papers to Hunter's *Georgical Essays*.

Markham, Gervase (?1568–1637) A prolific author, his works included many on agriculture and husbandry. It is thought that unscrupulous authors used his name and thus some of 'Markham's' writings were very unreliable. His knowledge of agriculture was based upon his years as a soldier in the Netherlands, where husbandry was considerably further advanced than in England.

Marshall, William (1745–1818) An agriculturalist who claimed four centuries of farming forebears, he became an agent on the Norfolk estate of Sir Harbord Harbord. In 1787, he began publication of his six-part survey of the agriculture of England. He proposed the establishment of a Board of Agriculture, but took no part in the Board county surveys. He retired to a Yorkshire estate in 1808, where he planned to establish an agricultural college but died before the plan was completed.

Meikle, Andrew (1719–1811) A Scottish millwright, he invented the threshing-machine in the form in which it was widely adopted. His threshing machine of 1784 was based upon a strong drum with fixed beating arms, thought to be an adaptation of a machine used for pulverizing flax. Although earlier machines had been known (from the 1730s onwards), they had all proved to have major flaws.

Pusey, Philip (1799–1855) An agriculturalist, he was also a dogged supporter of tenant rights in his capacity as a Member of Parliament and as a landowner. He was a member of the original committee for the foundation of the Royal Agricultural Society, the first editor of its Journal and was elected President in 1840, and again in 1853. He owned a 5,000-acre estate at Pusey, Berkshire, running his home farm in the most progressive manner. He introduced a system of water meadows and gave McCormick's reaper its first English trials on his land in 1851. He also rebuilt and improved the cottages of his labourers and provided them with allotments.

Townshend, Charles (Second Viscount, 1674–1738), known also as 'Turnip' Townshend. A diplomat who in his retirement, from 1730, turned enthusiastically to agriculture on his Norfolk estate at Rainham. His intro-duction of the turnip as a farm, rather than garden, crop revolutionized animal feeding as it was then possible to over-winter them, and made possible the work of men such as Bakewell. He also promoted other improvements such as the use of four-course crop rotation, including clover, and was enthusiastic over the benefits of enclosure.

Tull, Jethro (1674–1741) Farmer and writer, he perfected a method of machine-drilling for sowing seed. Foreign travels had given him the basis for his innovatory ideas and he carried out experiments at his Berkshire farm, 'Prosperous Farm', near Hungerford. When his writings appeared late in his life, they provoked various accusations of plagiarism.

Tusser, Thomas (*c.* 1520–80) A farmer and agricultural writer of whom it was said that nobody was 'better at the theory or worse at the practice of husbandry'. His *Hundreth Good Pointes of Husbandrie*, published in 1557, was written at a period when he was farming in Suffolk, where he had introduced the use of barley as a crop. This book was amplified to five hundred points in 1573; it was immensely popular, reissued and revised many times and still in print in the early 18th century. Only John Fitzherbert's *The Boke of Husbandry*, 1523, preceded it as a popular guide, and Tusser's work far surpassed the importance of Fitzherbert's.

Worlidge, John (*floreat* 1669–98) (usually wrote under the pseudonym, JW) A Hampshire man, his observations on all aspects of farming, including buildings, were published as *A Compleat System of Husbandry and Gardening*, etc. in 1716, the fifth edition of *Systema Agriculturae* which had first been published in 1669. Worlidge's book constituted the first systematic work on husbandry, replacing the folk-lore which had previously been the basis of agricultural knowledge.

Young, Arthur (1741–1821) A Suffolk-born agriculturalist he became, as a result of his own experiments in agriculture from 1763 onwards, secretary to the Board of Agriculture on its foundation in 1793. His innumerable publications include the Board of Agriculture reports for Suffolk, Essex, Hertfordshire and Oxfordshire. (His son, the Rev. Arthur Young, was author of the *General View* for Sussex). He began the *Annals of Agriculture* in 1784 which ran to forty-six volumes until its demise in 1809: among the contributors were King George III and Coke. He was familiar with all the leading figures in agriculture of his time; his visit to Bakewell was recorded by François de la Rochefoucauld (see bibliography). Young was largely responsible for the new scientific approach to agriculture, forerunning the so-called Agricultural Revolution.

Index